The Leadership Development Journey

The Leadership Development Journey

How Entrepreneurs Develop Leadership Through Their Lifetime

Jen Vuhuong

BEP BUSINESS EXPERT PRESS

The Leadership Development Journey: How Entrepreneurs Develop Leadership Through Their Lifetime

Copyright © Business Expert Press, LLC, 2018.

First published in 2018 by
Business Expert Press, LLC
222 East 46th Street, New York, NY 10017
www.businessexpertpress.com

ISBN-13: 978-1-94819-862-2 (paperback)
ISBN-13: 978-1-94819-863-9 (e-book)

Business Expert Press Entrepreneurship and Small Business Management Collection

Collection ISSN: 1946-5653 (print)
Collection ISSN: 1946-5661 (electronic)

Cover and interior design by Exeter Premedia Services Private Ltd., Chennai, India

First edition: 2018

10 9 8 7 6 5 4 3 2 1

Printed in the United States of America.

Dedicated to you, every great human being I meet every single day!

Abstract

This study reflects leadership development is a multilevel multicontext self-learning longitudinal journey embedded in a social learning environment with nine influential factors: parents, teamwork sport activities, teachers, role models, mentors/coaches, community-based networks (social factors); self-learning, experimentation, self-refection (self factors).

These findings of the book are based on a longitudinal qualitative study of interviewing 100 SME's founder-owner-managers and leaders attending a British leadership development framework and an international communication and leadership program.

Keywords

development in SME, entrepreneurial leadership, entrepreneurial, entrepreneurs, entrepreneurship, leadership development, leadership, personal development, SME engagement

Contents

Leadership Development Is a Lifetime Journey..xi

Chapter 1   The Journey of Leadership Literature 1
Chapter 2   Leadership in SMEs (Entrepreneurial Leadership) 19
Chapter 3   Leadership Development 29
Chapter 4   The Journey of the Research Methodology.....................37
Chapter 5   Leadership Development Journey Model of SME's
             Founder-Owner-Managers 41

Thanks Message to the Readers..95
Gratitude Moment...97
About the Author..99
Index 101

Leadership Development Is a Lifetime Journey

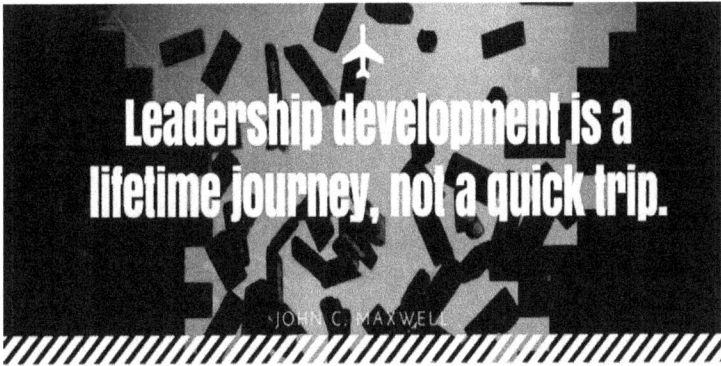

Leadership development is a lifetime journey, not a quick trip.

JOHN C. MAXWELL

The Twelve-Week Trip ...Facilitating For a Conscious Journey...

From January to April 2017, I had the opportunity to experience a 12-week course to study leadership as a part of my master's degree in International Management in the UK. Earlier to that, I always associated leadership with something big, just for someone in a big organization or a country, and ambiguous. The leadership perception wall was consciously and subconsciously socially constructed. Thanks to the 12 weeks, I founded each brick in the wall slowly taken down to open a diverse picture of leadership. Most importantly, it helped me embrace a strong desire to understand more about it. I would read about it, think about it, ask people about it everyday.

It seems that when we focus on something, opportunities start showing up. I was invited to be a speaker in a collaborative leadership conference. The lecturer of the leadership subject was also willing to guide me in the later leadership research. My journey of leadership development moved to the next chapter. After practicing leadership unconsciously and consciously over my whole life and deeply researching on the topic of leadership over the past year, writing this book to share with you what I think about and what I have found about the leadership development journey of a hundred SME's founder-owner-manager and future leaders from different countries has been an honor. The book aims to give you a clear big picture of different perspectives on leadership in literature/practice and the common patterns that help the interviewed leaders develop their leadership capability/identity in SMEs' context.

My intention is to convince you that leadership is not an ambiguous faraway subject but an act of developing, being, becoming, starting from TODAY, EVERYDAY; and that leadership resides in each and that everyone of us is a leader of our own life.

What Does Leadership Mean to Me?

This was the first question I asked myself in the first week of my leadership studying course. "Leadership is one of the most observed and least understood phenomena on earth" [1, 2, 3]. The statement hit me because I thought how much more attractive and ambiguous leadership would be until now. Every book I have read and every person I have met has a different interpretation of what leadership means, although Yulk [4] (cited in [5, 6, 7]) highlights, most assume that leadership involves influencing a person over others.

At the first week, I was not sure of the best way to define leadership if I were asked, which actually happened in the 12th week. My tutor's words were "…leadership is socially contextually constructed…" leveraging my thoughts to relate to the sense-making theory studied at the seventh week. The sense-making theory suggests that individuals decide what meaning to give and action to take upon events [8, 9, 10]. I realized it was not a matter of "the best definition" but the definition which is MEANINGFUL to each individual in daily life. I believe leadership for me is a journey toward my purpose of inspiring others. Although using a theory to define leadership is an action of choosing the best definition, the sense-making creates a feeling of having ownership of my lifetime journey and engages me in action toward my purpose.

I would like you also to take your own favorite definition, the definition that you resonate with the most, believe the most, trust the most, and, most importantly, take action upon it. And if you think it does not serve you, use the flexibility to change it for better because it is a journey—never ends, just getting better, EVERYDAY.

Where do you see (leadership)?

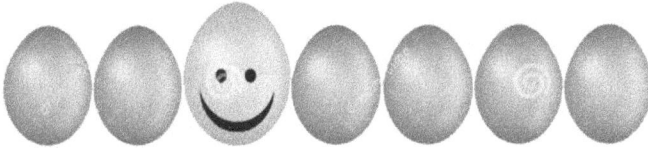

Most of us will answer the "biggest egg." The biggest egg is different—is the biggest one. What if other eggs do not line up there, the biggest egg is just a biggest egg? Everyone is a leader of themselves to create a leader in a social context.

Leadership comes from the "biggest egg" or maybe the act of lining up together?

Why "Everyone Is a Leader?"

Leadership studies have centered on individual leaders for organizations with a cross-sectional approach [3, 11, 12, 13]. Personally, I believe in the idea that leadership resides in each individual [14] and each individual is both a leader and a follower in different moments of life [15, 16]. I found that the leader-centric and heroics hold back individuals especially in developing countries to embark on their leadership potential. Most people would not think of themselves as leaders at least of their own life, even though they were top university students because society promotes "being heroic" leaders (e.g., the revolutionary leader—Lenin or CEOs—of big organizations such as Apple) instead of "being" and "becoming" leaders.

I had a friend named Paul who always believed in his leadership ability to make a difference in people's lives even though people told him he was unrealistic coming from the countryside. Nevertheless, Paul established a language center, which has helped to empower the voice of thousands becoming future leaders in Vietnam. Paul set a good example that leadership journey starts with believing in our ability of becoming a leader. And there are many more people like Paul that you and I can meet out there. Why don't you become one of them?

Why "Leadership Is a Journey?"

The idea of leadership as a process [3, 17] caught my attention in the second week. Day et al. [18] stated that leadership development is a continuous [19] and an ongoing process [20]. It reminded me of a humble answer from the senior leader, Bilimoria, the founder of Cobra-Beer, to my question on his leadership development journey "…I learn to lead everyday…" I reflected on my experience with Chevening (a British scholarship framework), which aims to embrace leadership development journey of future leaders [21]. Some of Chevening students shared with me that they never had leadership experience in any of the organizations before, but they convinced the scholarship panel by expressing their leadership potential through leading their lives and learning everyday.

As leadership is socially constructed [3], I consciously recognized that I was taught to make-sense of "leadership is a journey." Interestingly, that perception also resided at my subconscious level because when my lecturer asked my class in the first week "…when did you learn about leadership?" I spontaneously answered "everyday." The learning experience consciously and subconsciously influences individuals' behaviors [22], I consciously and subconsciously learned and enacted upon the idea that "leadership is a journey." This perception has guided my development journey so I would like you also to choose a perception that you trust and act upon that.

So What?

The answer for the "so what" question is the pinnacle of my story: to be open, learn from, and appreciate different perspectives and trust in the limitlessness of human potential. By drawing on different theories to explain my thoughts on my leadership studies journey, my intention is to praise the advantages of each perspective. There has been a call for an integrated theory that can encompass the many different aspects of leadership because one perspective alone cannot explain the complexity of leadership in the complex world [3]. By doing that, human being can reach our full potential and work in harmony together to create a positive change in life. I believe the ultimate goal of leadership studying is to increase our self-awareness with appreciation for the different perspectives and intention to contribute toward human/social development.

On the Quest for More Effective Way of Developing Leadership

The number of leadership courses and programs has expanded exponentially since the 1990s [23]. In 2012, $170 billion dollars was spent on leadership learning [24]. Despite the heavy investment, the effectiveness of leadership development program is often questioned [25, 26] due to its traditional approach.

Traditional leadership development programs promote the heroic views where "leaders are born" and most leadership development programs based on the traditional psychological approach focusing on leadership traits/competencies using classroom-based teaching methods [27]. This traditional approach fails to access the importance of different social actors as well as contexts, especially time dimension in the development process of an individual. Hence, most traditional leadership development programs do not provide the high-return investment because leadership is truly a development journey of becoming, not a trait. The modern world requires flexibility and continuous development. Research has shown primary areas of leadership failure: problems in interpersonal relationship, not meeting objectives, team leadership breakdowns, inability to adapt to transitions and changes. Transitions and changes are associated with a journey/process. The development process cannot be kept solely in a classroom context but in a social context.

This book reflects leadership development as a multilevel, multi-context, longitudinal social process, which suggests that leadership programs should have multilateral approaches integrated with social activities. This perspective is based on a longitudinal study of interviewing SME's founder-owner-managers and potential leaders attending a British leadership development framework and an international communication and leadership training program.

This book, hence, is structured as follows:

- The journey of leadership literature
- The journey of the research approach for this book
- The ultimate nine components of leadership development journey

This book is formed with an academic style that aims to fill the gap in leadership literature and propose a leadership development framework based on its narrative qualitative data.

References

[1] Burns, J.M. 1978. *Leadership*. New York, NY: Harper and Row.
[2] Morrill, R.L. 2010. *Strategic Leadership: Integrating Strategy and Leadership in Colleges and Universities*. Rowman & Littlefield Publishers.
[3] Schedlitzki, D., and G. Edwards. 2014. *Studying Leadership: Traditional and Critical Approaches*. Sage publications.
[4] Yukl, G., and C. Chavez. 2002. "Influence Tactics and Leader Effectiveness." *Leadership,* pp. 139–65.
[5] Gill, R. 2011. *Theory and Practice of Leadership*. Sage publications.
[6] Envy, R., and R. Walters. 2013. *Becoming a Practitioner in the Early Years*. Learning Matters.
[7] Workman-Stark, A.L. 2017. *Inclusive Policing from the Inside Out*. Springer.
[8] Weick, K.E. 1995. *Sensemaking in Organizations,* 3 vols. Sage.
[9] Pye, A., and A. Pettigrew. 2005. "Studying Board Context, Process and Dynamics: Some Challenges for the Future." *British Journal of Management* 16, pp. S27–38.
[10] Brown, A.D., I. Colville, and A. Pye. 2015. "Making Sense of Sensemaking in Organization Studies." *Organization Studies* 36, no. 2, pp. 265–77.
[11] Day, D.V., J.W. Fleenor, L.E. Atwater, R.E. Sturm, and R.A. McKee. 2014. "Advances in Leader and Leadership Development: A Review of 25 Years of Research and Theory." *The Leadership Quarterly* 25, no. 1, pp. 63–82.
[12] Dopson, S., E. Ferlie, G. McGivern, S. Behrens, and M.D. Fischer. 2016. "The Impact of Leadership and Leadership Development in Higher Education: A Review of the Literature and Evidence."

[13] Jian, G., and G.T. Fairhurst. 2016. "Leadership in Organizations." *The International Encyclopedia of Organizational Communication.*

[14] Kouzes, J.M., and B.Z. Posner. 2017. *A Coach's Guide to Developing Exemplary Leaders: Making the Most of the Leadership Challenge and the Leadership Practices Inventory (LPI).* John Wiley & Sons.

[15] Chartrand, T., W. Maddux, and J. Lakin. 2005. "Beyond the Perception-Behavior Link: The Ubiquitous Utility and Motivational Moderators of Nonconscious Mimicry." In *The New Unconscious,* eds. R. Hassin, J. Uleman and J. Bargh, 334–61. New York, NY: Oxford University Press.

[16] Sy, T., and T. McCoy. 2014. "Being Both Leaders and Followers: Advancing a Model of Leader and Follower Role Switching." *Followership: What Is It and Why Do People Follow.*

[17] Fleishman, E.A., M.D. Mumford, S.J. Zaccaro, K.Y. Levin, A.L. Korotkin, and M.B. Hein. 1991. "Taxonomic Efforts in the Description of Leader Behavior: A Synthesis and Functional Interpretation." *The Leadership Quarterly* 2, no. 4, pp. 245–87.

[18] Day, D.V. 2011. "Integrative Perspectives on Longitudinal Investigations of Leader Development: From Childhood Through Adulthood." *The Leadership Quarterly* 22, no. 3, pp. 561–71.

[19] Allen, S.J. 2007. "Adult Learning Theory & Leadership Development." *Leadership Review* 7, pp. 26–37.

[20] Day, D.V. 2000. "Leadership Development: A Review in Context." *The Leadership Quarterly* 11, no. 4, pp. 581–613.

[21] Chevening 2015. http://chevening.org/about-chevening

[22] Stoughton, C., R.H. Lupton, M. Bernardi, M.R. Blanton, S. Burles, F.J. Castander, A.J. Connolly, D.J. Eisenstein, J.A. Frieman, G.S. Hennessy, and R.B. Hindsley. 2002. "Sloan Digital Sky Survey: Early Data Release." *The Astronomical Journal* 123, no. 1, p. 485.

[23] Dugan, J.P., and S.R. Komives. 2007. *Developing Leadership Capacity in College Students.* College Park, MD: National Clearinghouse for Leadership Programs.

[24] Myatt, M. 2012. "The# 1 Reason Leadership Development Fails." *Forbes,* December 19.

[25] Day, D.V., and L. Dragoni. 2015. "Leadership Development: An Outcome-oriented Review Based on Time and Levels of Analyses." *Annu. Rev. Organ. Psychol. Organ. Behav* 2, no. 1, pp. 133–56.

[26] Petrie, N. 2014. "Vertical Leadership Development–Part 1 Developing Leaders for a Complex World." *Center for Creative Leadership.*

[27] Day, D.V., and S.M. Haipin. 2001. *Leadership Development: A Review of Industry Best Practices.* Army Research Inst Field Unit Fort Leavenworth KS.

CHAPTER 1

The Journey of Leadership Literature

Overview on Leadership Literature

Leadership is a choice.

—Stephen Covey

Leadership has been called "the most observed and least understood phenomena on earth"[1, 2]. Although being extensively studied for over almost a century, a universal definition for "what is leadership?" remains elusive [2, 3]. More than 30 years ago, in a review of leadership literature throughout his researching career [4], asserted that "there are almost as many definitions of leadership as there are persons who have attempted to define the concept" (p. 259). These different definitions fall into a number of the most recognized concepts such as traits, behaviors, and influence processes [3, 5]. Despite several definitions, most contemporary leadership researchers assume that leadership involves a person's influence over others to achieve a common goal [2, 3, 5, 6, 7] (Figure 1.1).

Common Goal

Influencing Process

Figure 1.1 A common way of defining leadership

Although leadership has been defined differently, literature on leadership has evolved from a static individualistic view to a dynamic socially constructed process that reflects the shifts in philosophical (from psychological to sociological), methodological (from quantitative to qualitative), and geographical aspect (from U.S. centric to European centric) [2, 8, 9] (see Figure 1.2 and Table 1.1). Psychologically driven scholars, mostly from the United States, focus on individual leaders' competencies. Hence, these scholars often employ a quantitative approach to assess "what" makes effective leaders (e.g., traits, skills, and styles). This approach forms the mainstream of leadership studies and contributes to understand leaders' characteristics and behaviors to predict the leadership effectiveness in their context [2, 8, 10].

However, an increasing number of sociologically driven scholars in the past two decades, especially from European continent, challenge the psychological approach for its individualistic static view on leadership that neglects the role of followership and the dynamics of context and social process [2, 8, 11]. Therefore, sociological studies (e.g., distributed leadership and relational approach) emphasize exploring "how" leadership is constructed within their complex processes and conditions [2, 10]. Although the nature of using a qualitative approach with a small number of leaders in most sociological studies does not allow them to be generalized or to be used to predict leadership effectiveness[2, 8]; this approach provides deeper understanding of the dynamic multilevel process of leadership, especially in the complex world.

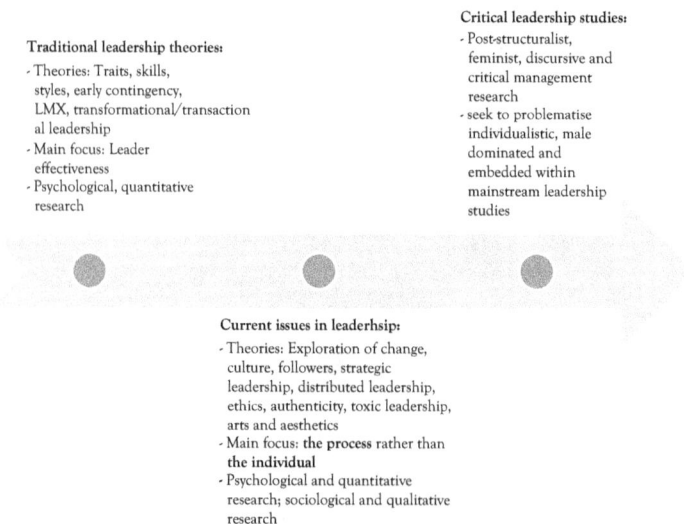

Traditional leadership theories:
- Theories: Traits, skills, styles, early contingency, LMX, transformational/transactional leadership
- Main focus: Leader effectiveness
- Psychological, quantitative research

Critical leadership studies:
- Post-structuralist, feminist, discursive and critical management research
- seek to problematise individualistic, male dominated and embedded within mainstream leadership studies

Current issues in leaderhsip:
- Theories: Exploration of change, culture, followers, strategic leadership, distributed leadership, ethics, authenticity, toxic leadership, arts and aesthetics
- Main focus: the process rather than the individual
- Psychological and quantitative research; sociological and qualitative research

Figure 1.2 A timeline of leadership studies (Based on [2])

Table 1.1 The main shifts in leadership studies (Based on [2])

Item	Traditional approach	Current issues	Critical studies
Timeline	Early 1990s–late 1990s	1990s onwards	Mid-2000s
Theories	• Leadership competencies: Traits, skills, styles • Contingency and LMX • Charismatic and transformational/ transactional leadership	• Leadership context • Followership, psychoanalytic and relational • Leadership and power • Strategic leadership • Distributed leadership • Leadership and culture • Leadership learning and development • Ethics, authenticity, toxic leadership, arts and aesthetics	• Post-structuralist, feminist, discursive and critical management research • Seek to problematize individualistic, male-dominated, and embedded within mainstream leadership studies
Focus	• Leadership effectiveness	• The process	• Critical issues
Research approach	• Psychological, quantitative research	• Psychological and quantitative research; sociological and qualitative research	• Mixed method

Paradigm shifts:
- Individual to *process*
- Masculine to *feminine*
- Westernize toward *cross-cultural leadership toward worldly (e.g., [9]) and inter- and intra-cultural*
- Psychological to *sociological*
- Leaders to *followers*
- Static to *dynamic*
- Objective to *subjective*

Shifting in aspects of philosophical, methodological and geographical:

- GEOGRAPHICAL: the United States (20th century), then European continent (the end of 20th century); cross-cultural leadership toward worldly (e.g., [9])

Despite the shifts, the mainstream of leadership studies has still under-represented the multilevel contextual variables [2] such as organizational size, culture, or group (e.g., gender) that influence leadership success [12,

13]. This expects future research to emphasize a process incorporating different contexts such as group or organizational size or individual cognitive scheme [2, 14, 15]. Hence, this book is based on a study emphasizing a sociological approach stressing leadership process and contextual variables to uncover the development journey of owner-managers of SMEs.

The following section describes the notable theories during the development journey of leadership literature.

Traditional Approaches to Leadership

Notable traditional leadership theories started from the early to late 1900s include traits, skills, styles, contingency, and transformational leadership [2, 3]. These studies follow the psychological quantitative approach and emphasize assessing leader effectiveness (Figure 1.3).

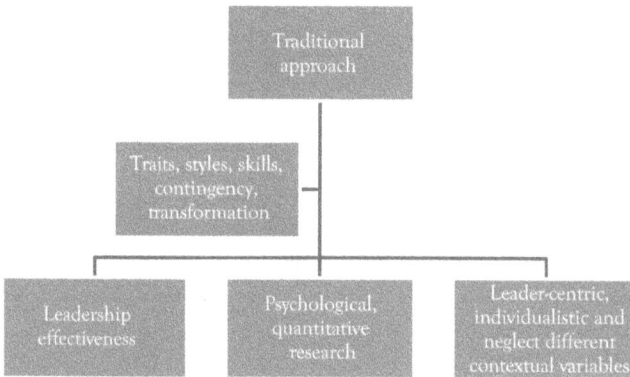

Figure 1.3 Traditional approaches to leadership

Traits

Trait theories come from "great man" theories [16] that consider "Leaders are born" [2, 17] and have been the longest-standing theories in leadership literature [3]. Trait leadership researchers (e.g., [17, 18]) investigate leaders' traits to distinguish them with non-leaders and predict leaders' competencies and effectiveness [8]. These traits vary from physical characteristics (e.g., height) and social backgrounds (e.g., education) to psychological factors (e.g., self-confidence) and social characteristics (e.g., cooperativeness) [8]. Despite the various findings, trait theories contribute to managerial effectiveness by providing particular character-istics needed to evaluate and recruit people for managerial or leadership roles [5]. However, trait theories neglect the interactions among leaders' traits with leaders' behaviors and situations [2, 8, 3]. This leads to further studies in leaders' skills and styles.

Styles and Skills Theories

While trait theories focus on leaders' characteristics, style and skill theories emphasize leaders' behaviors, either their styles, that is, the way they do things, or their skills, that is, their practiced ability [2]. In general, style studies fall into two categories: task concern versus people-concern and directive versus participative styles [6, 19] and skill studies orient toward three areas: problem, organization, and people [2, 20]. An often-cited study of Bass et al. [21] suggests five main leadership styles: directive, consultative, participative, negotiative, and delegative [2, 6]. A popular skill model [22, 23] poses three distinct skill sets of a manager or a leader in an organization: conceptual, human, and technical [2].

Although the findings in styles and skills are inconsistent, these studies contribute to the understanding of what behaviors of the leaders are most likely to influence their performance that have useful implications for leadership training [24].

Nevertheless, similar to trait theories, style and skill theories are crit-icized for excluding situational variances such as interaction of leaders' behaviors with followers [2, 8]. This leads to contingency leadership studies.

Contingency Leadership Theories

The lack of situational variances in traits, styles, and skills leadership studies promoted the contingency leadership studies in the late 1960s, 1970s, and 1980s [2]. The contingency studies argue that leadership effectiveness depends not only on individual leaders' traits or behaviors but also on the leadership situation [2, 25].

Most contingency theories (e.g., situational and path goal) emphasize leaders' ability to adapt to a situation (e.g., according to followers' character-istics), while Fieldler's theory argues that leadership styles are fixed. Study-ing in a special context—military, Fieldler's theory cannot be generalized

[2], but, together with other contingency theories, it contributes to the voice of situation and followership in shaping leadership. Hence, contingency theories also have implications for leadership training [3].

However, these inconsistent results have led to the loss of popularity of this approach over years [24, 25]. Moreover, this approach is also criticized for under-examining the level of interactions (e.g., dyadic and organization) between leaders' behaviors and situations as well as the impact of these behaviors on individual or group performance. This leads to transformational leadership, the most well-known approach in leadership studies.

Transformational Leadership

Transformational leadership was introduced by Bass [26] in the full-range leadership model, which has been the most widely used one [27, 28, 29]. In this model, transformational behavior is considered as the most active and effective leadership behavior compared to the other two behaviors, including transactional leadership and laissez-faire leadership [30].

Transformational leaders motivate and inspire followers to strive without external reward through four main behaviors: individualized consideration, intellectual stimulation, inspirational motivation, or idealized influence [2]. Hence, most researchers also suggest that transformational leadership behaviors positively impact on organizational performance through increasing job satisfaction and organizational commitments (e.g., [29, 31, 32]). This leads to the popular use of transformational leadership in leadership development[2]. Besides, this approach contributes to leadership literature by involving the followership and emotional aspects [2, 33]. However, post-heroic leadership scholars highlight different limitations of transformational leadership: lacking authenticity [34], increasing dependency in followers [35], excluding contextual variables, and being leader-centric [36, 37, 38].

The Shift Toward a Process Approach

Reviews for traditional leadership studies illustrate that although psychologically driven studies in leadership have progressed from leaders' competencies to leaders' behaviors considering situations and followers, these studies are still leader-centric, individualistic, and neglect different contextual variables such as organizational structure/culture or gender. Current studies especially sociologically driven studies emerging mostly from European continent in the last two decades have shifted leadership literature toward a distributed and socially constructed process [2, 8].

Distributed Leadership

Distributed leadership approach considers that leadership exists at all levels of organizations rather than solely on a few top executives unlike the traditional approach [2, 39] (Figure 1.4).

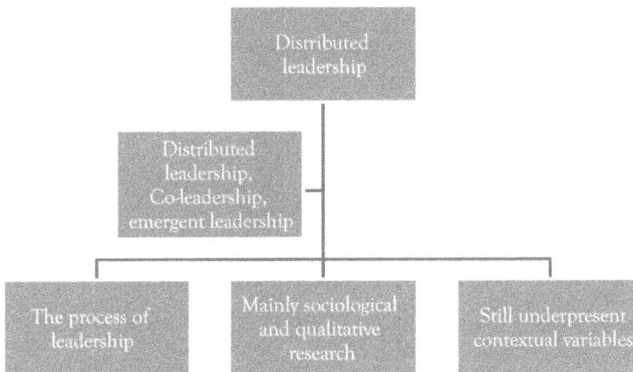

Figure 1.4 Distributed leadership

Distributed leadership can be found as far back as the 1920s but has only become mainstream in the past 20 years [39, 40]. Despite this recent popularity, in a meta-analysis of distributed leadership literature over the previous 20 years, Tian et al. [41] highlight its ambiguity in conceptualization and practice.

Conceptually, distributed leadership is seen in different theories such as dispersed leadership, shared leadership, co-leadership, and emergent leadership [2]. In practice, some researchers examine its favorable conditions (e.g., [42]) such as in community context (e.g., [43]), some evaluate the effects of its applications (e.g., [44, 45]), and some even critically assess the potential risks of its application regarding ethics (e.g., [46, 47]).

Although contributing to shift in leadership literature from individualistic to a distributed process, the fragmentation in distributed leadership studies reflects a similar limitation of traditional leadership studies in ineffectively incorporating contextual variables rigorously [2]. This reinforces the importance of enriching contextual variables in studying leadership, such as simultaneously assessing an individual or a group or organizational levels [41].

The Call for Emphasizing Contextual Variables

Although leadership literature has moved away from leader-centric to distributed, there has been a continuous call for future research to follow a process emphasizing contextual variables [2, 29, 37, 48, 14]. This promotes studies in leadership context (e.g., [14]) and in some underrepresented contexts such as in community context or small and medium enterprises (e.g., [38, 49, 50]).

Community Leadership

In response to the call for incorporating contextual variables into leadership study and the increasing number of communities, several researchers have changed their focus to examine leadership in the community context.

Community refers to village community, academic community, or business community [51, 52, 53, 54]. A community can be built based on location or relation. In particular, Taylor [55] suggests that a community has three core values: common beliefs and values, diverse relations, and reciprocity [52]. McMillan and Chavis [56], however, pose four dimensions of a community: membership, influence, reinforcement, and shared emotional connection. While Taylor [55] considers that individuals in a community share beliefs and values, McMillan and Chavis [56] emphasize the organic relationship in a community. Nevertheless, both the early approaches on community are criticized to be positivistic, which excludes the differences in beliefs and values of individuals [52, 57].

The differences of community and organizational contexts reflect ineffectiveness of using traditional leader-centric theories to approach community leadership [58, 59]. Community is less hierarchical, which implies that community leadership is relational rather than positional [54, 60]. In particular, an individual is perceived as a leader by the community members [61] through the roles of organizers or coordinators [58, 62, 63]. Hence, some researchers argue that complexity leadership theory (e.g., [64, 65]) fits with the flat structure in a community because the theory considers leaders as enablers rather than controllers as traditional leadership [54, 59, 66]. In the most recent community leadership research, Martiskainen [59] provides empirical evidence that leadership can be enhanced by being involved into social networks in energy community context.

Responding to the appreciation of community in shaping leadership, Edwards et al. [43] review the literature on distributed leadership and provide nine community concepts that exhibit distributed leadership: symbolism, a sense of belonging, a sense of community, individualism, values and ethics, language, dialect and discourse, liminality, and friendship. Although not using an empirical study approach, Edwards et al. [43] contribute a comprehensive framework that is theoretically and practically useful for understanding distributed leadership in community context.

Community is less hierarchical [54] and often based on volunteer actions[67], as a symbolism for change [68], involving the creation of social capital [59, 69], which are similar to entrepreneurial contexts. Although community leadership has been assessed with different leadership theories in different industries, such as education (e.g., [69, 70, 71]), health (e.g., [72]), politics (e.g., [68, 60]), tourism (e.g., [73]), energy [59],this is little evidence in profitable business contexts [74, 75]. Specifically, Gras et al. [74] suggest that the study of community as spaces and contexts for developing entrepreneurship has been neglected [75]. Moreover, [76, 77, 78] advocate that leadership literature underexamines the reinforcing relationship of leaders' reputations that result from leaders' behaviors or a community's reputation. This implies the importance of assessing how leadership is exercised differently in different individuals considering individual cognitive scheme (e.g., education and background), individual lived experiences, or national culture that are recommended in the context framework of Jepson [14].

Leadership Context

In responding to the continuing call for incorporating contextual variables more rigorously, several researchers focus on assessing different contextual variables in studying leadership. Two main perspectives follow the key debate between psychological (U.S.-centric) and sociological (European-centric) perspective [2]. Psychological perspective consists two main theories: implicit theory (e.g., [18]) and social identity (e.g., [79]).

While implicit theory considers individual cognitive scheme (e.g., background and education) influences perceiving and forming leadership, social identity theory suggests that social group's identity influences and is influenced by leadership. Implicit theory is criticized for neglecting the influence of group identity [80], while social identity theory is criticized for excluding individual cognitive scheme [37]. Although providing better understanding of leadership in the context of individual cognitive and group identity, empirical and conceptual psychology-driven research has not effectively studied the complexity and multilevel interaction of context between individual cognitive scheme and group identity [14, 81]. This leads to sociological perspective in studying leadership context.

To unravel the complexity and multilevel interaction within the context of leadership [81], provide empirical evidence that the immediate social context of an individual's department has the most influence on their understanding and practice of leadership. Broadening this finding, Jepson [14] proposes three dominant contextual levels that influence leadership practice in the research investigating understanding of leadership among 105 employees in 12 organizations in the UK and German chemical industries: (i) the immediate social (e.g., job), (ii) the general cultural (e.g., regional), and (iii) the historical or institutional context (e.g., education) [43] (see the following figure). Individuals categorize themselves in the interlinks between these contexts that shape their perception on leadership. Jepson [14] suggests that leadership researchers consider context simultaneously and dynamically instead of separating them. Although limited to the UK and German chemical industries, Jepson [14] provides a comprehensive model to assess leadership more rigorously. This model has also been appreciated in different contemporary leadership research (e.g., [2, 43, 82]).

Immediate social
Organisation
Department
Technology
Hierarchy
Industry
Job
Group

Institutional
History
Education
Regulation
Socialisation

Cultural
National
Organisational

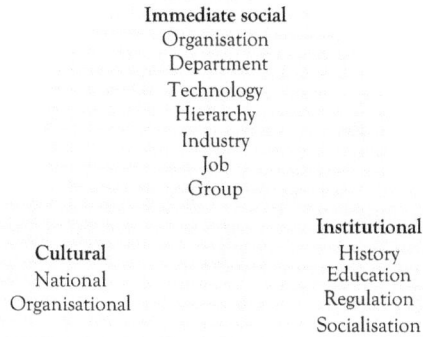

Figure 1.5 Context framework [14]

Hence, this book refers to Jepson's (2009a) [14] framework (see Figure 1.5) to assess richer contextual variables. In particular, this model's categories are referred to select potential candidates for the interview: (i) the immediate social (SMEs), (ii) the general cultural (British, European, American, Asian), and (iii) the historical or institutional context (experiencing in both being employed and running businesses).

References

[1] Burns, J.M. 1978. *Leadership*. New York, NY: Harper and Row.

[2] Schedlitzki, D., and G. Edwards. 2014. *Studying Leadership: Traditional and Critical Approaches*. Sage Publications.

[3] Northouse, P.G. 2017. *Introduction to Leadership: Concepts and Practice*. Sage Publications.

[4] Stogdill, R.M. 1974. *Handbook of Leadership: A Survey of Theory and Research*. Free Press.

[5] Yukl, G. 2011. "Contingency Theories of Effective Leadership." *The SAGE Handbook of Leadership*, pp. 286–98.

[6] Gill, R. 2011. *Theory and Practice of Leadership*. Sage Publications.

[7] Northouse, P.G. 2012. *Leadership: Theory and Practice*. Sage Publications.

[8] Jian, G., and G.T. Fairhurst. 2016. "Leadership in Organizations." *The International Encyclopedia of Organizational Communication*.

[9] Turnbull, S., P. Case, G. Edwards, D. Jepson, and P. Simpson. 2011. *Worldly Leadership: Alternative Wisdoms for a Complex World*. Palgrave.

[10] Collinson, D. 2011. "Critical Leadership Studies." *The SAGE Handbook of Leadership*, pp. 181–94.

[11] Collinson, D. 2017. "Critical Leadership Studies: A Response to Learmonth and Morrell." *Leadership* 13, no. 3, pp. 272–84.

[12] Hunter, S.T., K.E. Bedell-Avers, and M.D. Mumford. 2007. "The Typical Leadership Study: Assumptions, Implications, and Potential Remedies." *The Leadership Quarterly* 18, no. 5, pp. 435–46.

[13] Mayan, M., S. Lo, M. Oleschuk, A. Paucholo, and D. Laing. 2017. "Leadership in Community-Based Participatory Research: Individual to Collective." *Engaged Scholar Journal: Community-Engaged Research, Teaching, and Learning* 2, no. 2, pp. 11–24.

[14] Jepson, D. 2009a. "Leadership Context: The Importance of Departments." *Leadership & Organization Development Journal* 30, no. 1, pp. 36–52.

[15] Lovegrove, N., and M. Thomas. 2013. "Why the World Needs Tri-Sector Leaders." *Harvard Business Review* 13.

[16] Carlyle, T. 1866. *On Heroes, Hero-Worship, and the Heroic in History*. New York, NY: John Wiley.

[17] Stogdill, R.M. 1948. "Personal Factors Associated with Leadership: A Survey of the Literature." *The Journal of Psychology* 25, no. 1, pp. 35–71.

[18] Lord, R.G., R.J. Foti, and C.L. De Vader. 1984. "A Test of Leadership Categorization Theory: Internal Structure, Information Processing, and Leadership Perceptions." *Organizational Behavior and Human Performance* 34, no. 3, pp. 343–78.

[19] Wright, P.L. 1996. *Managerial Leadership*. London: Routledge.

[20] Mumford, M.D., S.J. Zaccaro, F.D. Harding, T.O. Jacobs, and E.A. Fleishman. 2000. "Leadership Skills for a Changing World: Solving Complex Social Problems." *The Leadership Quarterly* 11, no. 1, pp. 11–35.

[21] Bass, B.M., E.R. Valenzi, D.L. Farrow, and R.J. Solomon. 1975. "Management Styles Associated with Organizational, Task, Personal, and Interpersonal Contingencies." *Journal of Applied Psychology* 60, no. 6, p. 720.

[22] Burns, T. 1957. "Management in Action." *Operational Research Quarterly* 8, no. 2, pp. 45–60.

[23] Mann, F.C. 1965. "Toward an Understanding of the Leadership Role in Formal Organizations." *Leadership and Productivity*, pp. 68–103.

[24] Parry, K., and A. Bryman. 2006. "Leadership in Organizations." *The SAGE Handbook of Organization Studies*, p. 447.

[25] Yukl, G. 2011. "Contingency Theories of Effective Leadership." *The SAGE Handbook of Leadership* 24, no. 1, pp. 286–98.

[26] Bass, B.M. 1985. *Leadership and Performance Beyond Expectations*. New York, NY: The Free Press.

[27] Bono, J.E., A.C. Hooper, and D.J. Yoon. 2012. "Impact of Rater Personality on Transformational and Transactional Leadership Ratings." *The Leadership Quarterly* 23, no. 1, pp. 132–45.

[28] Westerlaken, K.M., and P.R. Woods. 2013. "The Relationship Between Psychopathy and the Full Range Leadership Model." *Personality and Individual Differences* 54, no. 1, pp. 41–46.

[29] Zaech, S., and U. Baldegger. 2017. "Leadership in Start-ups." *International Small Business Journal* 35, no. 2, pp. 157–777.

[30] Bass, B.M. 1995. "Theory of Transformational Leadership Redux." *The Leadership Quarterly* 6, no. 4, pp. 463–78.

[31] Avolio, B.J., W. Zhu, W. Koh, and P. Bhatia. 2004. "Transformational Leadership and Organizational Commitment: Mediating Role of Psychological Empowerment and Moderating Role of Structural Distance." *Journal of Organizational Behavior* 25, no. 8, pp. 951–68.

[32] Wang, H., A. Tsui, and K. Xin. 2011. "CEO Leadership Behaviors, Organizational Performance, and Employees' Attitudes." *The Leadership Quarterly* 22, no. 1, pp. 92–105.

[33] Koene, B.A., A.L. Vogelaar, and J.L. Soeters. 2002. "Leadership Effects on Organizational Climate and Financial Performance: Local Leadership Effect in Chain Organizations." *The Leadership Quarterly* 13, no. 3, pp. 193–215.

[34] Avolio, B.J., and W.L. Gardner. 2005. "Authentic Leadership Development: Getting to the Root of Positive Forms of Leadership." *The Leadership Quarterly* 16, no. 3, pp. 315–38.

[35] Ensley, M.D., C.L. Pearce, and K.M. Hmieleski. 2006a. "The Moderating Effect of Environmental Dynamism on the Relationship Between Entrepreneur Leadership Behavior and New Venture Performance." *Journal of Business Venturing* 21, no. 2, pp. 243–63.

[36] Edwards, G., and R. Gill. 2012. "Transformational Leadership Across Hierarchical Levels in UK Manufacturing Organizations." *Leadership & Organization Development Journal* 33, no. 1, pp. 25–50.

[37] Jackson, B., and K. Parry. 2011. *A Very Short Fairly Interesting and Reasonably Cheap Book About Studying Leadership.* Sage Publications.

[38] Leitch, C.M., and T. Volery. 2017. "Entrepreneurial Leadership: Insights and Directions." *International Small Business Journal* 35, no. 2, pp. 147–56.

[39] Holloway, J., A. Nielsen, and S. Saltmarsh. 2017. "Prescribed Distributed Leadership in the Era of Accountability: The Experiences of Mentor Teachers." *Educational Management Administration & Leadership*, 46, no. 4, pp. 538–55

[40] Bolden, R. 2011. "Distributed Leadership in Organizations: A Review of Theory and Research." *International Journal of Management Reviews* 13, no. 3, pp. 251–69.

[41] Tian, M., M. Risku, and K. Collin. 2016. "A Meta-analysis of Distributed Leadership from 2002 to 2013: Theory Development, Empirical Evidence and Future Research Focus." *Educational Management Administration & Leadership* 44, no. 1, pp. 146–64.

[42] Spillane, J.P., E.M. Camburn, and A. StitzielPareja. 2007. "Taking a Distributed Perspective to the School Principal's Workday." *Leadership and Policy in Schools* 6, no. 1, pp. 103–25.

[43] Edwards, G. 2011. "Concepts of Community: A Framework for Contextualizing Distributed Leadership." *International Journal of Management Reviews* 13, no. 3, pp. 301–12.

[44] Anderson, S.E., S. Moore, and J. Sun. 2009. "Positioning the Principals in Patterns of School Leadership Distribution." *Distributed Leadership According to the Evidence*, pp.111–36.

[45] Heck, R.H., and P. Hallinger. 2010. "Testing a Longitudinal Model of Distributed Leadership Effects on School Improvement." *The Leadership Quarterly* 21, no. 5, pp. 867–85.

[46] Lumby, J. 2013. "Distributed Leadership: The Uses and Abuses of Power." *Educational Management Administration & Leadership* 41, no. 5, pp. 581–97.

[47] Woods, P.A., and G.J. Woods. 2013. "Deepening Distributed Leadership: A Democratic Perspective on Power, Purpose and the Concept of the Self." *Leadership in Education (Vodenje v vzgoji in izobraževanju)* 2, pp. 17–40.

[48] Mumford, T.V., M.A. Campion, and F.P. Morgeson. 2007. "The Leadership Skills Strataplex: Leadership Skill Requirements Across Organizational Levels." *The Leadership Quarterly* 18, no. 2, pp. 154–66.

[49] Kempster, S., and J. Cope. 2010. "Learning to Lead in the Entrepreneurial Context." *International Journal of Entrepreneurial Behavior & Research* 16, no. 1, pp. 5–34.

[50] Leitch, C.M., C. McMullan, and R.T. Harrison. 2013. "The Development of Entrepreneurial Leadership: The Role of Human, Social and Institutional Capital." *British Journal of Management* 24, no. 3, pp. 347–66.

[51] Gusfield, J.R. 1975. *Community: A Critical Response*. New York, NY: Harper & Row.

[52] Edwards, G., and S. Turnbull. 2013. "A Cultural Approach to Evaluating Leadership Development." *Advances in Developing Human Resources* 15, no. 1, pp. 46–60.

[53] Walker, G., and P. Devine-Wright. 2008. "Community Renewable Energy: What Should It Mean?" *Energy Policy* 36, no. 2, pp. 497–500.

[54] Onyx, J., and R.J. Leonard. 2011. "Complex Systems Leadership in Emergent Community Projects." *Community Development Journal* 46, no. 4, pp. 493–510.

[55] Taylor, M. 1982. *Community, Anarchy and Liberty*. Cambridge University Press.

[56] McMillan, D.W., and D.M. Chavis. 1986. "Sense of Community: A Definition and Theory." *Journal of Community Psychology* 14, no. 1, pp. 6–23.

[57] Hooker, J.J., and M.E. Collinson. 2012. "Mammalian Faunal Turnover Across the Paleocene-Eocene Boundary in Nw Europe: The Roles of Displacement, Community Evolution and Environment." *Austrian Journal of Earth Sciences* 105, no. 1.

[58] Nowell, B., and N. Boyd. 2010. "Viewing Community as Responsibility as Well as Resource: Deconstructing the Theoretical Roots of Psychological Sense of Community." *Journal of Community Psychology* 38, no. 7, pp. 828–41.

[59] Martiskainen, M. 2017. "The Role of Community Leadership in the Development of Grassroots Innovations." *Environmental Innovation and Societal Transitions* 22, pp. 78–89.

[60] Bénit-Gbaffou, C., and O. Katsaura. 2014. "Community Leadership and the Construction of Political Legitimacy: Unpacking Bourdieu's 'Political Capital' in Post-Apartheid Johannesburg." *International Journal of Urban and Regional Research* 38, no. 5, pp. 1807–32.

[61] Dienesch, R.M., and R.C. Liden. 1986. "Leader-member Exchange Model of Leadership: A Critique and Further Development." *Academy of Management Review* 11, no. 3, pp. 618–34.

[62] Bryson, J.M., B.C. Crosby, and M.M. Stone. 2006. "The Design and Implementation of Cross-Sector Collaborations: Propositions from the Literature." *Public Administration Review* 66, pp. 44–55.

[63] Nowell, B., and N.M. Boyd. 2014. "Sense of Community Responsibility in Community Collaboratives: Advancing a Theory of Community as Resource and Responsibility." *American Journal of Community Psychology* 54, nos. 3–4, pp. 229–42.

[64] Keene, A., 2000. "Complexity Theory: The Changing Role of Leadership." *Industrial and Commercial Training* 32, no. 1, pp. 15–18.

[65] Uhl-Bien, M., R. Marion, and B. McKelvey. 2007. "Complexity Leadership Theory: Shifting Leadership from the Industrial Age to the Knowledge Era." *The Leadership Quarterly* 18, no. 4, pp. 298–318..

[66] Plowman, D.A., S. Solansky, T.E. Beck, L. Baker, M. Kulkarni, and D.V. Travis. 2007. "The Role of Leadership in Emergent, Self-Organization." *The Leadership Quarterly* 18, no. 4, pp. 341–56.

[67] Zanbar, L., and H. Itzhaky. 2013. "Community Activists' Competence: The Contributing Factors." *Journal of Community Psychology* 41, no. 2, pp. 249–63.

[68] Sullivan, H. 2007. "Interpreting' Community Leadership' in English Local Government." *Policy & Politics* 35, no. 1, pp. 141–61.

[69] Smith, L., and D. Riley. 2012. "School Leadership in Times of Crisis." *School Leadership & Management* 32, no. 1, pp. 57–71.

[70] Bukoski, B.E., T.C. Lewis, B.W. Carpenter, M.S. Berry, and K.N. Sanders. 2015. "The Complexities of Realizing Community: Assistant Principals as Community Leaders in Persistently Low-Achieving Schools." *Leadership and Policy in Schools* 14, no. 4, pp. 411–36.

[71] McKim, A.J., J.J. Velez, J. Stewart, and K. Strawn. 2017. "Exploring Leadership Development Through Community-Based Experiences." *Journal of Leadership Studies* 10, no. 4, pp. 6–16.

[72] Trapence, G., C. Collins, S. Avrett, R. Carr, H. Sanchez, G. Ayala, D. Diouf, C. Beyrer, and S.D. Baral. 2012. "From Personal Survival to Public Health: Community Leadership by Men Who Have Sex With Men in the Response to HIV." *The Lancet* 380, no. 9839, pp. 400–10.

[73] Cheuk, L.W., M.A. Nichols, M. Okan, T. Gersdorf, V.V. Ramasesh, W.S. Bakr, T. Lompe, and M.W. Zwierlein. 2015. "Quantum-gas Microscope for Fermionic Atoms." *Physical Review Letters* 114, no. 19, p. 193001.

[74] Gras, D., E. Mosakowski, and G.T. Lumpkin. 2011. "Gaining Insights from Future Research Topics in Social Entrepreneurship: A Content-Analytic Approach." In *Social and Sustainable Entrepreneurship*, 25–50. Emerald Group Publishing Limited.

[75] Cieslik, K. 2016. "Moral Economy Meets Social Enterprise Community-based Green Energy Project in Rural Burundi." *World Development* 83, pp. 12–26.

[76] Nowell, B., and L.M. Harrison. 2010. "Leading Change Through Collaborative Partnerships: A Profile of Leadership and Capacity Among Local Public Health Leaders." *Journal of Prevention & Intervention in the Community* 39, no. 1, pp. 19–34.

[77] Nowell, B., and N.M. Boyd. 2014. "Sense of Community Responsibility in Community Collaboratives: Advancing a Theory of Community as Resource and Responsibility." *American Journal of Community Psychology* 54, nos. 3–4, pp. 229–42.

[78] Nowell, B., A.M. Izod, K.M. Ngaruiya, and N.M. Boyd. 2016. "Public Service Motivation and Sense of Community Responsibility: Comparing Two Motivational Constructs in Understanding Leadership Within Community Collaboratives." *Journal of Public Administration Research and Theory* 26, no. 4, pp. 663–76.

[79] Ellemers, N., D. De Gilder, and S. Alexander Haslam. 2004. "Motivating Individuals and Groups at Work: A Social Identity Perspective on Leadership and Group Performance." *Academy of Management Review* 29, no. 3, pp. 459–78.

[80] Schyns, B., and J. Schilling. 2011. "Implicit Leadership Theories: Think Leader, Think Effective?" *Journal of Management Inquiry* 20, no. 2, pp. 141–50.

[81] Edwards, G., and D. Jepson. 2008. "Departmental Affiliation, Leadership and Leadership Development." In *Leadership Perspectives*, 144–60. Basingstoke, UK: Palgrave Macmillan.

[82] Jefferson, T., D. Klass, L. Lord, M. Nowak, and G. Thomas. 2014. "Context and the Leadership Experiences and Perceptions of Professionals: A Review of the Nursing Profession." *Journal of Health Organization and Management* 28, no. 6, pp. 811–29.

CHAPTER 2

Leadership in SMEs (Entrepreneurial Leadership)

Overview on Entrepreneurial Leadership Literature

Although there is extensive literature on leadership, most studies were conducted by corporations and there are still some unrepresented contexts such as small and medium-sized enterprises ("SMEs") [1]. Leadership study in SMEs ("entrepreneurial leadership") has garnered much attention since the early 1990s due to an increasing number of entrepreneurs [2]. However, literature on entrepreneurial leadership is fragmented both conceptually and practically [2, 3, 4], because entrepreneurial leadership scholars use different existing theories [2] including leadership theories that have been highlighted to be fragmented, scattered by different leadership scholars (e.g., [4, 5]). Moreover, the topic is still elusive, especially the process of how entrepreneurs develop their leadership remains nascent [2, 7] (Figure 2.1).

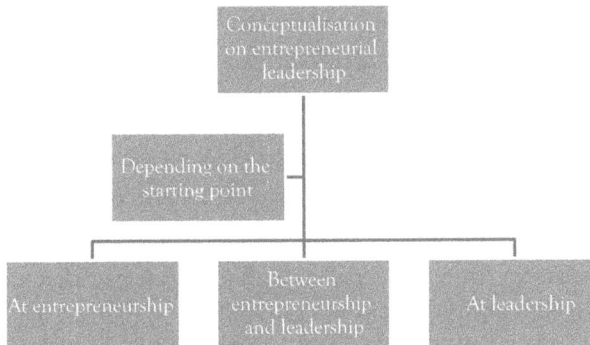

Figure 2.1 Conceptualization on entrepreneurial leadership

Table 2.1 The three views on entrepreneurial leadership

View	Key statements	Authors
First view: at leadership		
	Leadership and entrepreneurship overlap in areas of people and task abilities	Perren and Burgyone [8]
	It is more cogent and parsimonious to view entrepreneurship as simply a type of leadership that occurs in a specific setting…one that is not beyond the reach or understanding of available theory in the areas of leadership and interpersonal influence	Vecchio [9]
	Four shared characteristics of entrepreneurship and leadership: vision, influence, creativity, and planning	Cogliser and Brigham [10]
Second view: at entrepreneurship		
	Entrepreneurial leadership creates visionary scenarios that are used to assemble and mobilize a supporting cast of leaders who become committed to the discovery and exploitation of strategic value creation	Gupta et al. [11]
	A set of similar "characteristics" common to both leaders and entrepreneurs: vision, problem-solving, decision making, risk taking, and strategic initiatives	Fernald et al. [12]
	Entrepreneurial leadership is a unique concept combining the identification of opportunities, risk taking beyond security, and being resolute enough to follow through	Kuratko [13]
Third view: existing between entrepreneurship and leadership		
	Entrepreneurial leadership is the leadership role performed in entrepreneurial ventures, rather than in the more general sense of an entrepreneurial style of leadership	Leitch et al. [1]
	Entrepreneurial leadership entails influencing and directing the performance of group members toward the achievement of organizational goals that involve recognizing and exploiting entrepreneurial opportunities	Renko et al. [14]

Conceptually, researchers can be grouped into one of the three viewpoints of entrepreneurial leadership depending on their starting point: (i) at leadership (entrepreneurship is a type of leadership), (ii) at entrepreneurship (entrepreneurship is the essence of leadership), or (iii) at entrepreneurial leadership (entrepreneurial leadership is a new paradigm existing at the intersection of entrepreneurship and leadership) (Table 2.1).

From the first viewpoint, researchers consider entrepreneurial leadership in a specific context of SMEs that can be well explained through traditional leadership theories and research (e.g., [8, 9]). For example, Vecchio [9] argues that entrepreneurship and leadership have several overlapped patterns such as behaviors (risk-taking propensity, need for achievement, need for autonomy, self-efficiency) and unrepresented topics such as followership.

Although providing an understanding of entrepreneurial leadership based on the extensively studied topic of leadership, this view inherits the limitation of leadership studies by being leader-centric and individualistic [15]. Moreover, leadership theories may ineffectively assess the dynamics, ambiguity, risk, and uncertainty of entrepreneurial context [16], because most of the studies are conducted in a static context [2, 4, 15].

Researchers of the second viewpoint also define the common themes between leadership and entrepreneurship but emphasize entrepreneurship as the essence of leadership in the entrepreneurial context(e.g., [2, 11, 12]). Most researchers of this viewpoint associate entrepreneurial leadership with vision and value creation, reflecting the definition of Gupta et al. [11], "entrepreneurial leadership creates visionary scenarios that are used to assemble and mobilise a supporting cast of leaders who become committed to the discovery and exploitation of strategic value creation" (p. 242) [2]. Competencies of different entrepreneurs are also identified by these researchers, for instance, Fernald et al. [12] highlight five characteristics of entrepreneurs including vision, problem solving, decision making, risk taking, and strategic initiatives. Although enriching literature on entrepreneurial leadership from the dynamic of entrepreneurial context, the second viewpoint shares the same limitation of the first view in being entrepreneur-centric.

Researchers of the third viewpoint consider entrepreneurial leadership as a new paradigm in the intersection between entrepreneurship and leadership to benefit from both fields(e.g., [1, 2, 17, 18]). For instance, Leitch et al. [1] define that entrepreneurial leadership is "leadership role performed in entrepreneurial ventures, rather than in the more general sense of an entrepreneurial style of leadership" (p. 348). Leitch and Volery [2] particularly illustrate the three main reasons for exploring entrepreneurial leadership through the interaction between entrepreneurship and leadership by summarizing the findings of the three main viewpoints on entrepreneurial leadership literature.

First, different researchers state that entrepreneurs are leaders by definition (e.g., [12, 19]). For example, Kempster and Cope [19] posit that "entrepreneurs are leaders by virtue of their position, being encouraged to take this role through organizational necessity" (p. 27). Second, the literature on entrepreneurship literature reflects that of leadership literature in emphasizing individual competencies (e.g., [20, 21]). Third, entrepreneurial leadership, entrepreneurship, and leadership share similar styles such as being authentic [22] and the most common style is transformational (e.g., [2, 7, 14]). Although not providing empirical evidence, Leitch and Volery [2] present a comprehensive summary of different viewpoints on entrepreneurial leadership that highlights the major benefits of the third perspective.

Hence, this book considers that entrepreneurial leadership lies in the interaction of entrepreneurship and leadership to access the literature in both viewpoints (Table 2.2).

The Evolution of Entrepreneurial Leadership Literature

Table 2.2 The evolution on entrepreneurial leadership literature [2]

View	Findings	Authors
(i) Psychological		
Traits	Entrepreneurs with leadership roles are single-minded, thick-skinned, dominating individuals, and unlike managers	Brockhaus [23]; Nicholson [24]
Competencies	Entrepreneurial leadership is formed by functional competencies (operations, finance, marketing, and human resources) and self-competencies (intellectual integrity, utilizing external advisors and creating a sustainable organization)	Swiercz and Lydon [25]
Behaviors	Different behaviors due to interaction indifferent contexts: disrupt existing patterns through embracing uncertainty and creating controversy, encourage novelty by allowing experiments and supporting collective action, provide sense making and sense giving through the artful use of language and symbols, and stabilize the system by integrating local constraint	Lichtenstein and Plowman [26]
Leadership-behaviors and performance	Authentic leadership is a significant positive predictor for job satisfaction, work happiness, and organizational commitment	Jensen and Luthans [22]
	Transformational leadership is a significant positive predictor for venture growth	Ensley, Hmieleski, and Pearce [27]

	Transformational leadership is a significant positive predictor for the creativity of followers	Gumusluoglu and Ilsev [28]
Distributed leadership	Distributed leadership between top management team with capacity for sensemaking and problem-solving	Cope et al. [29]
(ii) Contextual variables emphasize		
Context	Context as a moderator of entrepreneurial leadership behaviors	Antonakis and Autio [17]
Social process	Entrepreneurial leadership development as a social process comprising different activities, events, and exchanges over time (comprising developing identity—a sense of self—and a capacity for social interaction—a sense of others)	Leitch et al. [30]
Dynamic context	Multilevel factors (i.e., philosophical traditions and cultural values and organizational, personal, and transitional factors) form a complex and dynamic context of entrepreneurial leadership	Wang et al. [31]
Social capital	The development of skills, knowledge, and abilities of leaders only occurs through the development of their social capital	Leitch et al. [1]
Becoming process	The development of leadership capability reflects a complex social process of becoming	Kempster and Cope [19]
(iii) Critical issues		
Ethics	Findings: sustaining entrepreneurial leadership for value creation necessitates ethical action to build legitimacy Criticism: philosophical approach does not take into account the extent to which different societies encourage such experimentation	Surie and Ashley [32]
Genders	Emphasize the importance of genders in studying entrepreneurial leadership studying	Harrison et al. [33]
Special issue		
Incorporating different traditional theories	Transformational leadership has significant positive influence on start-up performance through communicating an inspiring vision and facilitating their development and growth, while transactional and laissez-faire do not	Zaech and Baldegger [7]
Critical view (feminist view)	Entrepreneurial leader identity is social constructed, multifaceted, diverse, and potentially conflicting	Dean and Ford [34]
Co-action in developing entrepreneurial leadership	Entrepreneurial leadership emerges from the co-action (the intersection between the field of entrepreneurship and leadership) of a venture's leaders	Sklaveniti [35]

Apart from sharing a fragmented pattern in conceptualization, literature on entrepreneurial leadership has experienced a similar evolution to that on leadership: from static psychological (competencies to behaviors) to sociological dynamic views stressing contextual variables. This again highlights the use of leadership theories in studies related to entrepreneurial leadership, leading to similar limitations [2].

Specifically, the research on entrepreneurial leadership is mainly driven by a psychological approach focusing on the "what" of entrepreneurial leadership rather the "how" of its development [2, 4]. For example, Nicholson [24] suggests the traits that distinguish entrepreneurial leaders from other leaders and non-leaders are high risk-taking behavior, openness, achievement orientation, and low deliberation. Swiercz and Lydon [25] posit that entrepreneurial leaders have functional competencies (operations, finance, marketing, and human resources) and self-competencies (intellectual integrity). Although these studies have implications in recruitment or training, they are entrepreneur-/leader-centric that fail to incorporate the contextual dynamic process of entrepreneurial leadership.

In responding to the need for assessing the how-to dynamic for the developmental process of entrepreneurial leadership, contemporary entrepreneurial leadership researchers emphasize the sociological approach, although the numbers remain few. Of these, Kempster and Cope [19] apply a qualitative study with an interpretative phenomenological analysis approach to explore leadership learning of lived experiences. They suggest that leadership learning reflects informal and contextual social processes for becoming a leader, echoing with that of a previous study by Kempster [36]. However, they argue that an entrepreneurial context creates a specific crucible for entrepreneurs to learn to lead through situated leadership patterns and relationships rather than the apprenticeship learning process of employed managers, as reported by Kempster [36]. Although not specifying the change in leadership development overtime (e.g., skills and styles) or incorporating contextual variables such as gender, that study highlights the importance of assessing entrepreneurial leadership, learning, and development at the multiple levels of lived experiences.

Complementing the research by Kempster and Cope [19], Leitch et al. [1] examined the entrepreneurial leadership development process through the levels of lived experiences. They suggest that entrepreneurial leadership is a social process that focuses on human capital (enhancing leader's skills, knowledge) but only occur in social capital development process (peer-to-peer interaction, trust building). Although still not incorporated at institutional or group level, such as gender, their study reinforced the need to access the entrepreneurial leadership development in informal social contexts.

Responding to the voice of gender issues, Dean and Ford [34] use a narrative inquire (life history) approach to access the change of perception toward 16 female entrepreneurs and found that their perceptions change overtime. These perceptions are constructed through community, daily activities, or lived experiences. In spite of not involving male leaders, their study challenges the masculine voice in the mainstream of literature on entrepreneurial leadership and once again highlights the role of different contexts such as individuals, lived experiences, and community.

Although these few research hold the limitation of a qualitative approach, they contribute to deeper understanding of the entrepreneurial leadership development processes that often occur in informal multilevel contexts such as lived experiences, social factors, or community. This calls for more research on the leadership development processes in the entrepreneurial context [2].

References

[1] Leitch, C.M., C. McMullan, and R.T. Harrison. 2013. "The Development of Entrepreneurial Leadership: The Role of Human, Social and Institutional Capital." *British Journal of Management* 24, no. 3, pp. 347–66.

[2] Leitch, C.M., and T. Volery. 2017. "Entrepreneurial Leadership: Insights and Directions." *International Small Business Journal* 35, no. 2, pp. 147–56.

[3] Ruvio, A., Z. Rosenblatt, and R. Hertz-Lazarowitz. 2010. "Entrepreneurial Leadership Vision in Nonprofit vs. for-profit Organizations." *The Leadership Quarterly* 21, no. 1, pp. 144–58.

[4] Volery, T., S. Mueller, and B. von Siemens. 2015. "Entrepreneur Ambidexterity: A Study of Entrepreneur Behaviours and Competencies in Growth-oriented Small and Medium-sized Enterprises." *International Small Business Journal* 33, no. 2, pp. 109–29.

[5] Jian, G., and G.T. Fairhurst. 2016. "Leadership in Organizations." *The International Encyclopedia of Organizational Communication*.

[6] Schedlitzki, D., and G. Edwards. 2014. *Studying Leadership: Traditional and Critical Approaches*. Sage Publications.

[7] Zaech, S., and U. Baldegger. 2017. "Leadership in Start-ups." *International Small Business Journal* 35, no. 2, pp. 157–777.

[8] Burgoyne, J.G., and L. Perren. 2002. The Management and Leadership Nexus: Dynamic Sharing of Practice and Principle.

[9] Vecchio, R.P. 2003. "Entrepreneurship and Leadership: Common Trends and Common Threads." *Human Resource Management Review* 13, no. 2, pp. 303–27.

[10] Cogliser, C.C., and K.H. Brigham. 2004. "The Intersection of Leadership and Entrepreneurship: Mutual Lessons to be Learned." *The Leadership Quarterly* 15, no. 6, pp. 771–99.

[11] Gupta, V., I.C. MacMillan, and G. Surie. 2004. "Entrepreneurial Leadership: Developing and Measuring a Cross-cultural Construct." *Journal of Business Venturing* 19, no. 2, pp. 241–60.

[12] Fernald, L.W., Jr., G.T. Solomon, and A. Tarabishy. 2005. "A New Paradigm: Entrepreneurial Leadership." *Southern Business Review* 30, no. 2, p. 1.

[13] Kuratko, D.F. 2007. "Entrepreneurial Leadership in the 21st Century: Guest Editor's Perspective." *Journal of Leadership & Organizational Studies* 13, no. 4, pp. 1–11.

[14] Renko, M., A. El Tarabishy, A.L. Carsrud, and M. Brännback. 2015. "Understanding and Measuring Entrepreneurial Leadership Style." *Journal of Small Business Management* 53, no. 1, pp. 54–74.

[15] Roomi, M.A., and P. Harrison. 2011. "Entrepreneurial Leadership: What Is It and How Should It Be Taught?" *International Review of Entrepreneurship*.

[16] Gartner, W.B., N.M. Carter, and P.D. Reynolds. 2010. "Entrepreneurial Behavior: Firm Organizing Processes." In *Handbook of Entrepreneurship Research*, 99–127. New York, NY: Springer.

[17] Antonakis, J., and E. Autio. 2007. "Entrepreneurship and Leadership." *The Psychology of Entrepreneurship*, pp.189–207.

[18] Cogliser, C.C., and K.H. Brigham. 2004. "The Intersection of Leadership and Entrepreneurship: Mutual Lessons to be Learned." *The Leadership Quarterly* 15, no. 6, pp. 771–99.

[19] Kempster, S., and J. Cope. 2010. "Learning to Lead in the Entrepreneurial Context." *International Journal of Entrepreneurial Behavior & Research* 16, no. 1, pp. 5–34.

[20] Cunningham, J.B., and J. Lischeron. 1991. "Defining Entrepreneurship." *Journal of Small Business Management* 29, no. 1, p. 45.

[21] Chen, M.H. 2007. "Entrepreneurial Leadership and New Ventures: Creativity in Entrepreneurial Teams." *Creativity and Innovation Management* 16, no. 3, pp. 239–49.

[22] Jensen, S.M., and F. Luthans. 2006. "Entrepreneurs as Authentic Leaders: Impact on Employees' Attitudes." *Leadership & Organization Development Journal* 27, no. 8, pp. 646–66.

[23] Brockhaus, R.H. 1982. *The Psychology of the Entrepreneur.*

[24] Nicholson, N. 1998. "Personality and Entrepreneurial Leadership: A Study of the Heads of the UK's Most Successful Independent Companies." *European Management Journal* 16, no. 5, pp. 529–39.

[25] Swiercz, P.M., and S.R. Lydon. 2002. "Entrepreneurial Leadership in High-tech Firms: A Field Study." *Leadership & Organization Development Journal* 23, no. 7, pp. 380–89.

[26] Lichtenstein, B.B., and D.A. Plowman. 2009. "The Leadership of Emergence: A Complex Systems Leadership Theory of Emergence at Successive Organizational Levels."

[27] Ensley, M.D., C.L. Pearce, and K.M. Hmieleski. 2006a. "The Moderating Effect of Environmental Dynamism on the Relationship Between Entrepreneur Leadership Behavior and New Venture Performance." *Journal of Business Venturing* 21, no. 2, pp. 243–63.

[28] Gumusluoglu, L., and A. Ilsev. 2007. "Transformational Leadership, Creativity, And Organizational Innovation." *Journal of Business Research* 62, no. 4, pp. 461–73.

[29] Cope, J. 2011. "Entrepreneurial Learning from Failure: An Interpretative Phenomenological Analysis." *Journal of Business Venturing* 26, no. 6, pp. 604–23.

[30] Leitch, C.M., F.M. Hill, and R.T. Harrison. 2010. "The Philosophy and Practice of Interpretivist Research in Entrepreneurship: Quality, Validation, and Trust." *Organizational Research Methods* 13, no. 1, pp. 67–84.

[31] Wang, H., A. Tsui, and K. Xin. 2011. "CEO Leadership Behaviors, Organizational Performance, and Employees' Attitudes." *The Leadership Quarterly* 22, no. 1, pp. 92–105.

[32] Surie, G., and A. Ashley. 2008. "Integrating Pragmatism and Ethics in Entrepreneurial Leadership for Sustainable Value Creation." *Journal of Business Ethics* 81, no. 1, pp. 235–46.

[33] Harrison, R., C. Leitch, and M. McAdam. 2015. "Breaking Glass: Toward a Gendered Analysis of Entrepreneurial Leadership." *Journal of Small Business Management* 53, no. 3, pp. 693–713.

[34] Dean, H., and J. Ford. 2017. "Discourses of Entrepreneurial Leadership: Exposing Myths and Exploring New Approaches." *International Small Business Journal* 35, no. 2, pp. 178–96.

[35] Sklaveniti, C. 2017. "Processes of Entrepreneurial Leadership: Co-acting Creativity and Direction in the Emergence of New SME Ventures." *International Small Business Journal* 35, no. 2, pp. 197–213.

[36] Kempster, S. 2006. "Leadership Learning Through Lived Experience: A Process of Apprenticeship?" *Journal of Management & Organization* 12, no. 1, pp. 4–22.

CHAPTER 3

Leadership Development

Overview on Leadership Development Literature

The importance of leadership to organization competitiveness has gathered much attention from researchers of leadership development over the past two decades [1, 2]. Leadership development studies have experienced a similar pattern as leadership studies, which shift from a psychological to sociological view [2, 3]. Traditional psychologically driven researchers focus on a leader's competencies (e.g., [4, 5]), while contemporary sociologically driven researchers consider leadership as a social process for becoming a leader (e.g., [6]) or for identity development (e.g., [7, 8]).

The shift in leadership development literature also reflects the regular application of traditional leadership theories to leadership development [2, 3]. By reviewing leadership development studies over the previous 25 years, Day et al. [3] particularly highlight that traditional leadership theories unsuccessfully contribute to the leadership development practice. In particular, these theories are individualistic and cross-sectional and they neglect contextual variables, while leadership development is an inherent contextually longitudinal process [3, 9, 10]. Therefore, future leadership development studies are expected to focus on the development process and incorporate a contextual, multilevel, and longitudinal approach [3, 10].

Hence, this book emphasizes a contextual, multilevel, and processual approach toward leadership development.

Traditional Leadership Development Approach

Static Approach

Table 3.1 Intrapersonal perspective (Based on Day et al. [3])

View	Findings	Authors
Experience and leaning	A leader's level of experience plays a role in determining how much he or she will learn; however, not all leaders learn at the same pace or in the same way	Hirst et al. [4]
Skills	As leaders assume more senior positions in an organization, acquisition of strategic and business skills will be vital for effective performance than acquisition of interpersonal and cognitive skills	Mumford et al. [5]
	Effective leadership entails developing and integrating wisdom, intelligence, and creativity	Sternberg [11]
	Identity, meta-cognition, and self-regulation processes are crucial to the refinement of knowledge structures and information processing capabilities associated with leadership expertise	Lord and Hall [12]
Self-development	Orientation of work, mastery, and career growth facilitate a leader's self-development activities	Boyce et al. [13]
	Specific organizational-level (i.e., human resources practices) and group-level (i.e., supervisor style) constructs can promote leader self-development	Reichard and Johnson [14]
Self-efficiency	Leader developmental efficacy, or one's belief in his/her ability to develop leadership knowledge or skills, is theorized to predict engagement and success in leader development	Reichard et al. [15]
Mindset	Leaders must change their thinking process—they should use their minds to implement business processes within an organization	Jeseviciute-Ufartiene et al. [16]
Moral	Leadership development model in Western context is not applicable to Vietnam and China as the focus of a Vietnamese leader's self-development is centered on improving their moral standards	Ren et al. [17]

The traditional approach in leadership development is mainly associated with experience and learning, skills, self-development, or self-efficiency, or as Day et al. [3] call, "intrapersonal perspective." This approach is the main stream of leadership development literature and still remains active (e.g., [2, 15]) (see Table 3.1 above). This approach aims to assess what factors influence developing leaders or leadership. Researchers highlight different factors influencing leadership development: experience and individual differences [4]; strategic and business skills [5]; wisdom, intelligence, creative [11]; work orientation, mastery orientation, and career-growth orientation [13]. Although contributing to the understanding of the factors predicting the process of "leaders" development, the studies driven by intrapersonal factors fail to explore the process of "leadership" development. In particular, personality is constant, while the development process is dynamic[3]. Moreover, this approach ignores leadership's behaviors and its interactions with followers, leading to interpersonal approach [3].

Interpersonal-driven research contributes to the missing parts in intrapersonal approach by examining leadership behaviors through social mechanisms such as mentoring, leadership training, and job assignments for leadership development [18]. Day et al. [3] do not consider training as an ideal method because the development process is long term and dynamic, while training is often short term and conceptual. Moreover, while training is more suited to solve known problems, contemporary leaders are faced with complex ambiguity. Some interpersonal-driven researchers also assess the relationship of leadership behaviors and followers. A majority suggest that it is important to develop authentic leadership behaviors due to its positive impact on followers and their performance (e.g., [19, 20, 21]). However, they do not clarify how followers perceive their leaders as authentic. Steffens et al. [22] provide empirical evidence that leaders are perceived as authentic when they are true to the collective identity of the group they lead. Although not elucidating how leaders could develop their identities to match with the collective identity of their groups, the finding of Steffens et al. [22] suggests the importance of incorporating social identity in studying leadership development that leads to socially processual-driven studies.

Process Approach

It can be seen that intrapersonal and interpersonal studies contribute to predict the factors of developing effective leaders but fail to explain the process of how to develop these factors [3]. Hence, more contemporary studies emphasize the development process of leadership such as 360-degree feedback [23] or leadership as identity [7, 8].

A popular theory, 360-degree feedback, uses feedback as a process of development [24]. In particular, giving feedback to a leader will result in behavioral change and, ultimately, improvement in organizational performance [25]. Warech et al. [23] suggest that leaders who are high self-monitors do not receive higher 360-degree feedback ratings. Hooijberg and Choi [26], however, argue that effectiveness may lie in the eye of the beholder (or evaluator). Despite its contribution to incorporating different perspectives, 360-degree feedback is criticized owing to lack of contextual variables and social processes such as individual or organizational situations [3].

In responding to the call for incorporating social processes within leadership development, various contemporary researchers approach leadership development as "identity development" (e.g., [7, 12]). Identity is often referred "to an individual's self-definition based on a relatively stable set of meanings associated with a particular role [10, 27]." Therefore, identity impacts individuals' self-perception and their perception others as leaders [12] and that can be influenced through reading or social interactions [7]. It is suggested that having leader identity motivates individuals to seek opportunities to exercise and enhance their leadership capabilities [10, 28]. However, Kempster and Cope [29] posit that the nine successful entrepreneurs interviewed in their study have low-salience leadership identity in contrast to the findings in the employed managers of Kempster [30]. This suggests the importance of specifying the research context in approaching identity development.

Little empirical evidence is found to investigate the development process of leadership identity in a specific context and its change overtime [10, 31]. In a most recent study on leadership development in a grassroot-innovations community, Miscenko et al. [10] provide empirical evidence that leadership development changes in both skills and identity overtime. Their study highlights the importance of discovering leadership development with different perspectives (both identity and skills) overtime in a social context such as community [3, 32].

Hence, this book emphasizes covering different leadership development outcomes such as skills and identity overtime to obtain the multi aspects of leadership development.

Calls for Future Research of Leadership Development

It can be seen that leadership development has progressed from a psychological approach to a sociological approach emphasizing the developmental process of leadership. However, the mainstay of leadership development is still individualistic, while leadership development is a multilevel process occurring at different levels of individuals, groups, organizations, and society [3, 9]. Moreover, most research is conducted in formal organizational contexts, while the developmental process can start from the informal context, such as a family [33] or community [10], which suggests the importance of examining both formal and informal settings [34, 35]. Besides, despite the shift toward a social process of becoming a leader or toward identity development, the change overtime of different aspects of leadership outcomes such as skills and identity remains neglected [10, 36].

The Quest for a Broad Study

The literature review in leadership, entrepreneurial leadership, and leadership development reveals a set of contexts for the current study.

First, leadership literature has called for future research moves toward a sociological approach emphasizing processual and contextual variables. Second, leadership in small and medium enterprises (SMEs) remains an underrepresented area and little evidence found in entrepreneurial leadership literature explores how entrepreneurs develop their leadership overtime. Third, the literature on leadership development has called for future research to focus on processual and relational variables emphasizing contextual variables in both formal and formal settings. Specifically, literature of leadership context suggests identifying a specific context by simultaneously assessing different contextual variables: (i) the immediate social (e.g., job), (ii) the general cultural (e.g., regional), and (iii) the historical or institutional context (e.g., education).

Hence, this study aims to assess the leadership development journey of owner-managers in SMEs context incorporating other contextual variables such as social factors and lived experiences. The contexts built upon the literature review guide this study's interview questions, which can be categorized into three key aspects: *(i) What are the main factors influencing a leader's leadership development? (ii) How do these factors influence a leader's leadership development? (iii) Which aspects of a leader's leadership development are influenced by each factor?* These three key questions are articulated throughout a leader's lifetime from childhood to current positions. Vertically, this study simultaneously assesses multilevel contextual variables (SMEs context, individual leader's cognitive schema, social factors, and lived experiences) as well as multilevel leadership development outcomes (e.g., skills and identity). With these objectives, the study's methodology is discussed in the following section.

References

[1] Guillén, L., M. Mayo, and K. Korotov. 2015. "Is Leadership a Part of Me? A Leader Identity Approach to Understanding the Motivation to Lead." *The Leadership Quarterly* 26, no. 5, pp. 802–20.

[2] Schedlitzki, D., and G. Edwards. 2014. *Studying Leadership: Traditional and Critical Approaches.* Sage Publications.

[3] Day, D.V., J.W. Fleenor, L.E. Atwater, R.E. Sturm, and R.A. McKee. 2014. "Advances in Leader and Leadership Development: A Review of 25 Years of Research and Theory." *The Leadership Quarterly* 25, no. 1, pp. 63–82.

[4] Hirst, G., L. Mann, P. Bain, A. Pirola-Merlo, and A. Richver. 2004. "Learning to Lead: The Development and Testing of a Model of Leadership Learning." *The Leadership Quarterly* 15, no. 3, pp. 311–27.

[5] Mumford, T.V., M.A. Campion, and F.P. Morgeson. 2007. "The Leadership Skills Strataplex: Leadership Skill Requirements Across Organizational Levels." *The Leadership Quarterly* 18, no. 2, pp. 154–66.

[6] Kempster, S., and J. Stewart. 2010. "Becoming a Leader: A Co-produced Autoethnographic Exploration of Situated Learning of Leadership Practice." *Management Learning* 41, no. 2, pp. 205–19.

[7] Ford, J., N. Harding, and M. Learmonth. 2008. *Leadership as Identity: Constructions and Deconstructions.* Springer.

[8] Ford, J. 2010. "Studying Leadership Critically: A Psychosocial Lens on Leadership Identities." *Leadership* 6, no. 1, pp. 47–65.

[9] Day, D.V. 2011. "Integrative Perspectives on Longitudinal Investigations of Leader Development: From Childhood Through Adulthood." *The Leadership Quarterly* 22, no. 3, pp. 561–71.

[10] Miscenko, D., H. Guenter, and D.V. Day. 2017. "Am I a Leader? Examining Leader Identity Development Over Time." *The Leadership Quarterly*.

[11] Sternberg, R.J. 2008. "The WICS Approach to Leadership: Stories of Leadership and the Structures and Processes that Support Them." *The Leadership Quarterly* 19, no. 3, pp. 360–71.

[12] Lord, R.G., and R.J. Hall. 2005. "Identity, Deep Structure and the Development of Leadership Skill." *The Leadership Quarterly* 16, no. 4, pp. 591–615.

[13] Boyce, L.A., R. Jeffrey Jackson, and L.J. Neal. 2010. "Building Successful Leadership Coaching Relationships: Examining Impact of Matching Criteria in a Leadership Coaching Program." *Journal of Management Development* 29, no. 10, pp. 914–31.

[14] Reichard, R.J., and S.K. Johnson. 2011. "Leader Self-development as Organizational Strategy." *The Leadership Quarterly* 22, no. 1, pp. 33–42.

[15] Reichard, R.J., D.O. Walker, S.E. Putter, E. Middleton, and S.K. Johnson. 2017. "Believing Is Becoming: The Role of Leader Developmental Efficacy in Leader Self-development." *Journal of Leadership & Organizational Studies* 24, no. 2, pp. 137–56.

[16] Jeseviciute-Ufartiene, L. 2014. "Importance of Planning in Management Developing Organization." *Journal of Advanced Management Science* 2, no. 3.

[17] Ren, S., N. Collins, and Y. Zhu. 2014. "Leadership Self-development in China and Vietnam." *Asia Pacific Journal of Human Resources* 52, no. 1, pp. 42–59.

[18] Galli, E.B., and G. Müller-Stewens. 2012. "How to Build Social Capital with Leadership Development: Lessons from an Explorative Case Study of a Multi business Firm." *The Leadership Quarterly* 23, no. 1, pp. 176–201.

[19] Avolio, B.J., and W.L. Gardner. 2005. "Authentic Leadership Development: Getting to the Root of Positive Forms of Leadership." *The Leadership Quarterly* 16, no. 3, pp. 315–38.

[20] Aydin, S., and N. Kaya. 2016. "Authentic Leadership in Sales Management: The Effects on Salespeople's Task Related Outcomes." *Business and Economic Research* 6, no. 2, pp. 133–55.

[21] Regan, S., H.K. Laschinger, and C.A. Wong. 2016. "The Influence of Empowerment, Authentic Leadership, and Professional Practice Environments on Nurses' Perceived Inter professional Collaboration." *Journal of Nursing Management* 24, no. 1, pp. E54–61.

[22] Steffens, N.K., F. Mols, S.A. Haslam, and T.G. Okimoto. 2016. "True to What We Stand for: Championing Collective Interests as a Path to Authentic Leadership." *The Leadership Quarterly* 27, no. 5, pp. 726–44.

[23] Warech, M.A., J.W. Smither, R.R. Reilly, R.E. Millsap, and S.P. Reilly. 1998. "Self-monitoring and 360-degree Ratings." *The Leadership Quarterly* 9, no. 4, pp. 449–73.

[24] Seifert, C.F., and G. Yukl. 2010. "Effects of Repeated Multi-source Feedback on the Influence Behavior and Effectiveness of Managers: A Field Experiment." *The Leadership Quarterly* 21, no. 5, pp. 856–66.

[25] Waldman, D.A., L.E. Atwater, and D. Antonioni. 1998. "Has 360 Degree Feedback Gone Amok?" *Academy of Management Perspectives* 12, no. 2, pp. 86–94.

[26] Hooijberg, R., and J. Choi. 2000. "Which Leadership Roles Matter to Whom? An Examination of Rater Effects on Perceptions of Effectiveness." *The Leadership Quarterly* 11, no. 3, pp. 341–64.

[27] Stryker, S., and P.J. Burke. 2000. "The Past, Present, and Future of an Identity Theory." *Social Psychology Quarterly*, pp. 284–97.

[28] Day, D.V., M.M. Harrison, and S.M. Halpin. 2012. *An Integrative Approach to Leader Development: Connecting Adult Development, Identity, and Expertise*. Routledge.

[29] Kempster, S., and J. Cope. 2010. "Learning to Lead in the Entrepreneurial Context." *International Journal of Entrepreneurial Behavior & Research* 16, no. 1, pp. 5–34.

[30] Kempster, S. 2006. "Leadership Learning Through Lived Experience: A Process of Apprenticeship?" *Journal of Management & Organization* 12, no. 1, pp. 4–22.

[31] Day, D.V., and L. Dragoni. 2015. "Leadership Development: An Outcome-oriented Review Based on Time and Levels of Analyses." *Annu. Rev. Organ. Psychol. Organ. Behav.* 2, no. 1, pp. 133–56.

[32] DeRue, D.S. 2011. "Adaptive Leadership Theory: Leading and Following as a Complex Adaptive Process." *Research in Organizational Behavior* 31, pp. 125–50.

[33] Murphy, S.E., and S.K. Johnson. 2011. "The Benefits of a Long-lens Approach to Leader Development: Understanding the Seeds of Leadership." *The Leadership Quarterly* 22, no. 3, pp. 459–70.

[34] Carroll, B.J. 2016. "Leadership as Identity." *Leadership-as-Practice: Theory and Application*, p. 91.

[35] Edwards, G., and S. Turnbull. 2013. "A Cultural Approach to Evaluating Leadership Development." *Advances in Developing Human Resources* 15, no. 1, pp. 46–60.

[36] Martiskainen, M. 2017. "The Role of Community Leadership in the Development of Grassroots Innovations." *Environmental Innovation and Societal Transitions* 22, pp. 78–89.

CHAPTER 4

The Journey of the Research Methodology

This book is based on a qualitative study across two periods. It goes with my journey of being involved in a British government leadership development as well as a year of studying for my master's degree in the UK.

The study explores the leadership development journey of founder-owner-managers of small and medium enterprises (SME) throughout their lifetime. To achieve this objective, the study employs a narrative interpretive constructivist qualitative approach.

There are two main steps of the study: *(i) interviewed SME's owner-managers to build a model demonstrating the development process; (ii) interviewed leaders of a one-year leadership development program that lasted one year to test the model.*

Philosophies and Approaches

The objective of this study is to explore the leadership development journey of SME's owner-managers, which implies a social constructivism view. Constructivism or social constructivism (or often described as interpretivism) considers individuals' subjective worldview and make meaning from the world they live in [1, 2, 3]. In particular, they "develop subjective meanings of their experiences—meanings directed toward certain objects or things" [4]. Hence, using an interpretivism world view allows the researcher to examine how SME's founder-owner-managers develop their leadership through their lived experiences.

Moreover, the interpretive world view allows the researcher to involve in the data collection process, which is important because the researcher is a co-creator of the narrative when interpreting leaders' narratives [5, 6]. Furthermore, interpretive world view is subjective in that it promotes the varying perspectives of different leaders, which allows the involvement of different leaders [7, 8, 9].

The study's objective of "*How leaders in SMEs develop their leadership throughout their lifetime?*" indicates that quality approach is suitable. In particular, qualitative approach has four main advantages: (i) understanding the meaning that leaders give to their experiences and the influence of their interpretation on their behaviors; (ii) understanding the context and its influence on leaders' action and behaviors (e.g., how entrepreneurial context influenced leaders' leadership behaviors); (iii) understanding the processes by which action and behaviors take place (e.g., leadership development processes); (iv) the data analysis process is inductive that helps generate new theories (e.g., leadership development journey of SMEs leaders) [10, 11, 12, 13].

Qualitative approach is usually not used to generate results since it is used to obtain rich information of a small number of leaders [10]. This study employs a qualitative approach to obtain rich information of the leaders instead of generalizing the results. Therefore, the quantitative or the mixed method (quantitative and qualitative) is not appropriate for this study. Moreover, quantitative approach, which is used to collect quantified data [9, 10], is not appropriate for the present study because the study aims to explore lived experiences of leaders, which cannot be quantified.

Research Strategy

Among other strategies such as grounded theory, ethnography, case studies, and phenomenological [6, 7, 14], narrative strategy is most suitable for research that aims to capture lived experiences of individuals. Hence, a narrative inquiry strategy complements the interpretive qualitative approach in exploring the leadership journey of SME leaders. Moreover, this study focuses on contextual variables in shaping leadership, and a narrative inquiry allows researchers to involve contextual variables such as individual's biography (e.g., jobs and hometown), culture (e.g., radical or ethnic), history (e.g., time and place), and emotions [10, 15]. Furthermore, a narrative inquiry offers the flexibility in collecting data from different sources such as observation, documents, and other sources, even though interview is often the primary data source [14, 16, 17]. This allows the present study to incorporate both formal and informal data, which has been suggested to be important to leadership development process [18, 19].

Interview Process

The First Interview Period

Fifty participants who are founder-owner-manager of 50 different SMEs were interviewed.

The main question is *How do SME's founder-owner-managers develop their leadership throughout their lifetime?* There are three main parts of the interview questions:

1. Opening questions lasting 5 to 10 minutes to establish connection and put leaders at ease as well as gain understanding on the foundation of leaders' leadership approach.
2. Main questions lasting 60 to 90 minutes to investigate the leadership development journey throughout the leaders' life time. With the support of a timeline diagram capturing influential factors on leader's leadership development journey, three main questions are articulated in each stage (e.g., childhood, employment) of leaders' journey.
   (i) *What are the main factors influencing a leader's leadership development?*
   (ii) *How do these factors influence a leader's leadership development?*
   (iii) *Which aspects of a leader's leadership development are influenced by each factor?*
3. Small talk to let leaders freely express any other experiences as well as clarify any ambiguous information.

The Second Interview Period

After finishing the first interview period, data was analyzed to create a leadership development framework. A second interview was taken place to interview 50 people attending in the leadership development program Chevening and Toastmasters.

(Chevening is a British government full scholarship providing opportunities to students to study one-year master's degree in the UK. Chevening has a comprehensive diversity program for students to enhance their leadership and networking skills.)

(http://chevening.org/partners/benefits)

(Toastmasters is an platform teaching and developing communication and leadership skills.)

(https://toastmasters.org/about/who-we-are)

References

[1] Lincoln and Guba (1994).

[2] Lincoln, Y.S., S.A. Lynham, and E.G. Guba. 2011. "Paradigmatic Controversies, Contradictions, and Emerging Confluences, Revisited." *The Sage Handbook of Qualitative Research* 4, pp. 97–128.

[3] Mertens, D.M. 2014. *Research and Evaluation in Education and Psychology: Integrating Diversity with Quantitative, Qualitative, and Mixed Methods.* Sage Publications.

[4] Creswell, J.W., and C.N. Poth. 2017. *Qualitative Inquiry and Research Design: Choosing Among Five Approaches.* Sage Publications.

[5] Riessman, C.K. 1993. *Narrative Analysis*, 30 vols. Sage Publications.

[6] Riessman, C.K. 2008. *Narrative Methods for the Human Sciences.* Sage Publications.

[7] Creswell and Poth (2017).

[8] Maxwell, J.A. 2008. "Designing a Qualitative Study." *The SAGE Handbook of Applied Social Research Methods* 2, pp. 214–53.

[9] Saunders, M.N. 2011. *Research Methods for Business Students,* 5th ed. Pearson Education India.

[10] Creswell (2013).

[11] Daymon, C., and I. Holloway. 2010. *Qualitative Research Methods in Public Relations and Marketing Communications.* Routledge.

[12] Merriam, S. 2009. *Qualitative Research: A Guide to Design and Implementation.* San Fransisco: John Willey & Sons.

[13] Silverman, D., ed. 2016. *Qualitative Research.* Sage Publications.

[14] Daiute, C. 2014. *Narrative Inquiry: Dynamic Narrating in Life and Research.*

[15] Clandinin, D.J., and F.M. Connelly. 2000. *Narrative Inquiry: Experience and Story in Qualitative Research.*

[16] Bauer, M. 1996. *The Narrative Interview.* LSE Methodology Institute Papers.

[17] Creswell (2017).

[18] Carroll, B.J. 2016. "Leadership as Identity." *Leadership-as-Practice: Theory and Application*, p. 91.

[19] Edwards, G., and S. Turnbull. 2013. "A Cultural Approach to Evaluating Leadership Development." *Advances in Developing Human Resources* 15, no. 1, pp. 46–60.

CHAPTER 5

Leadership Development Journey Model of SME's Founder-Owner-Managers

The leadership development journey in this study is a self-development process embedded in a social learning environment. The study found nine influential factors on leadership development:

- **Social factors**: parents, teamwork sport activities, teachers, role models, mentors/coaches, community-based networks
- **Self factors**: self-learning, experimentation, self-reflection

Individuals learn from social factors that influence their self factors or vice versa. Social factors influence individuals through processes of observation, being told, being disciplined, involving, and creating. The leadership development outcomes include identity, skills, behaviors, and perceptions. The whole development process is influenced by contextual factors such as gender, time, and age (Figure 5.1).

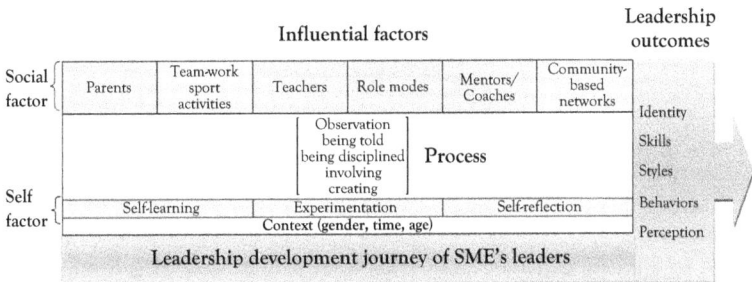

	Influential factors						Leadership outcomes
Social factor	Parents	Team-work sport activities	Teachers	Role modes	Mentors/ Coaches	Community-based networks	Identity
			Observation being told being disciplined involving creating		Process		Skills
							Styles
Self factor	Self-learning		Experimentation		Self-reflection		Behaviors
	Context (gender, time, age)						Perception
	Leadership development journey of SME's leaders						

Figure 5.1 Leadership development journey framework of SME's founder-owner-manager

Table 5.1 Factors of leadership development journey of SME's founder-owner

	Developing process	Influential factors	Leadership outcomes	The drives of the journey
Social process	Observing, Being told, Being disciplined, Role modeling, Mentoring, Coaching, Feedback	Parents, Teachers, Role models, Mentors/coaches Community-based social networks, Children	Perception Traits Behaviors Skills Styles Identity	Purpose, Decision
Self-process	Reading/listening Experimentation Reflection/ Making sense			
Contexts (the immediate social, the general cultural, and the historical or institutional context)				

Leadership Influential Factors

Social Factors

Parents and Teachers

> *Children learn to smile from their parents.*
>
> —Shinichi Suzuki

This study shows evidence that during childhood, family—especially parents—significantly influences leadership qualities, in particular, hard-work quality through observational learning processes or instilling process or involving process (Figure 5.2).

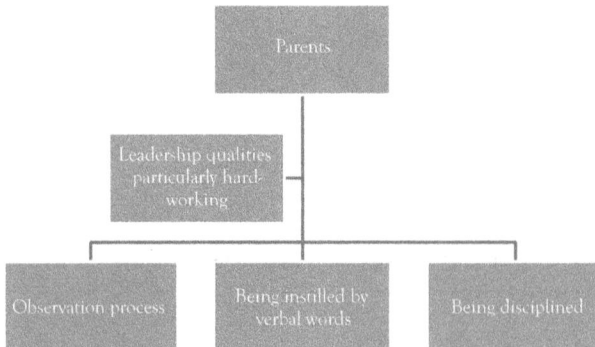

Figure 5.2 The influence process of parents

Leadership Quality, Especially Hardwork Learned from Parents

Although each leader in this study recalled different leadership qualities that they learned from their parents (such as positivity, independence, inspiration, and hardworking), hardwork emerged as the most common learned quality in most leaders.

Social learning theory [1] states that individuals observe and replicate the behaviors (e.g., leadership and aggression) of their role models, who are often their parents, if these behaviors create positive outcomes [2]. The leaders interviewed in the study replicated the hardwork behavior of their parents, and hardwork is a quality of successful entrepreneurs [3, 4]. For example, Poku stated that he observed the quality of hardwork of his mum, "Of course my mum. I think she is exceptionally hard-working, very humble. I know everybody will talk about their mum but even if she was directly trying to preach that to us or not, we got it, we saw that in action." Paul H learned the hardworking quality by not only observing but also being directly disciplined by his parents since he was a kid "you didn't go to bed at night and so you're either exhausted or you've done everything that you need to do."

The Pitfalls of Parent's Influence

While no leaders associated uncomfortable feelings toward their mother's influences, some leaders did associate such feelings toward their father's behaviors. For example, with an uneasy feeling, Jo stated her ambition was triggered by her father's expectation of her:

> That comes from my dad. When I was 8 years old, he said to me, what did you want to do when you when you grow up, and I said "I want to be Prime Minister. So, he said to me at 8 'that's a really good start, what are you going to do after that?" That sounds like a really positive thing to say, but for an 8-year-old kid, it was like bloody hell, yeah what's on earth do I have to do to please you?

While some females tend to be driven by their fathers' expectation, some males wanted to outdo their fathers because their fathers were not ambitious. For example, Ben said, "My dad is a person I aspire not to be. He is not ambitious, not communicative."

Such findings partially support a previous finding by Kirkwood [5] and Kempster and Cope [6], in which fathers have dominant influence on leaders and some male entrepreneurs desire independence from their fathers or to outdo them. However, while Kirkwood [5] suggests that some female entrepreneurs look up to their fathers for advice, this study shows that some female leaders are driven by their father's expectation of them, but there is an uncomfortable expression toward these behaviors. This suggests the importance of how parents communicate their expectations to their children (Figure 5.3).

How to have effective parenting styles—authoritative parents?

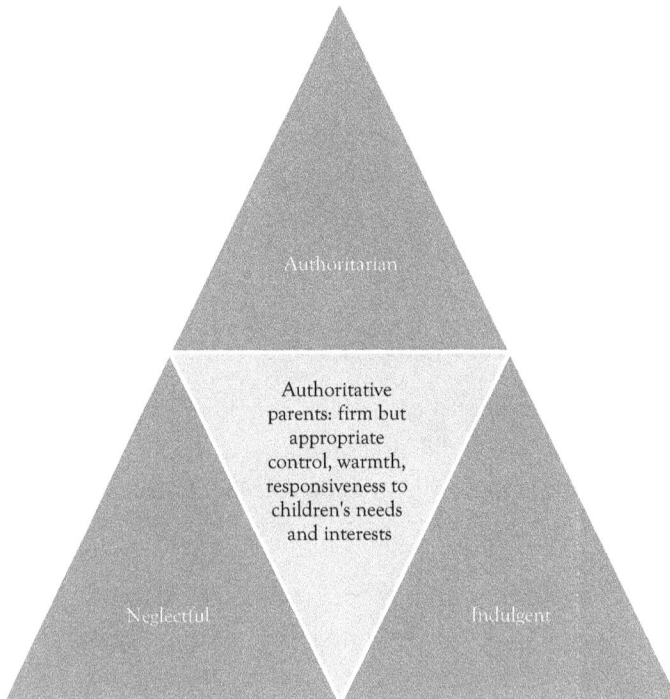

Figure 5.3 Parenting styles

Previous research such as Santrock [7] suggested that there are four types of parenting styles: authoritarian, neglectful, indulgent, and authoritative [8]. The study also supports the previous finding where authoritative parenting embrace self-regulated, socially responsible, and cognitively competent in children [9, 10, 11, 12]. *Authoritative* parenting has also been associated with early entrepreneurial competence in high school students and business founders [13]. Moreover, this study suggests that family members with authoritative styles exhibit strongly that they can become role models for children to follow the styles.

Authoritative parenting in the developmental psychology literature is characterized by firm but appropriate control along with high levels of warmth or responsiveness to children's needs and interests [9]. Authoritative parenting increases the self-efficacy in children. Self-efficacy is defined as one's belief in one's ability to accomplish given tasks [14] that is necessary for leadership positions [15] because those who assume leadership roles must firmly believe in the goals and in their abilities. Popper et al. [16] observed a clear the link between self-efficacy, or a generalized belief in one's ability to perform a wide variety of tasks, and the ability to lead.

Arvey et al. [17, 18] state that only approximately 30 percent of leader emergence can be attributed to genetic factors, leaving a considerable amount of variance not explained by genetic influence per se. This leads to the consideration of other social factors in the leadership development journey of leaders (Figure 5.4).

Teamwork Activities

Unity is strength... when there is teamwork and collaboration, wonderful things can be achieved.

—Mattie Stepanek

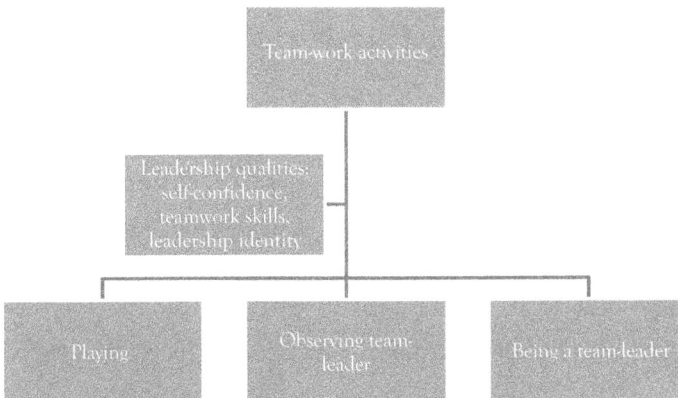

Figure 5.4 The influence process of team-work activities

Apart from family, this study found that playing sports or leading sports teams significantly and positively influence a leader's leadership development, particularly in increasing their self-confidence, competitiveness, teamwork, or leadership identity. Such findings partially support Murphy and John's [19] research, which suggests that sports-related skills in early ages are transferable to leadership development in adulthood, for example: people skills [20], confidence [21], self-efficacy, and competitiveness [22].

The findings also differ from previous research, which suggests that sports have a potentially negative impact that reflects on one's self-image [23], which is the feeling of having no social competence [24] and difficulty communicating with people outside of sports teams [25]. These contrasting findings in these previous researches may result from differences in individuals or team positions, and the present empirical study shows the influence of these differences on leadership development.

This study found that the leaders significantly influenced by sports are top performers and even captains of their sports teams. Another leader, Caroline, had an uneasy time recalling the influence of sports on her leadership development as she was not the captain but easily recalled her leadership identity being shaped from leading her Young Entrepreneurship team. It seems that the leadership abilities or identity learned from sports may have also resulted from feeling successful in some aspects and/or being recognized by having a chance to lead a team rather than solely the sports itself. Kim [26] suggests that team captains exhibit better leadership capability than non captains, while Huntrods et al. [27] argue that there is no clear difference in team captains and non captains in acquiring leadership positions.

Although not providing enough evidence to conclude that high-level performers are more significantly influenced by sports than low-level performers in leadership development, this study rather suggests that having opportunities to lead teams gives individuals the opportunities for exercising their leadership ability and styles and shaping their leadership identity. Hence, sports and teamwork activities should be incorporated in leadership programs and more children should be given the opportunity to lead in schools to embrace their leadership potential. Moreover, individual differences (levels of sports performance) and team position differences should be considered in leadership research and leadership development programs.

Teachers

> *A good teacher can inspire hope, ignite the imagination, and instill a love of learning*
>
> —Brad Henry

Teachers' interaction with students emphasized the way of interacting with others. For example, Paul P mentioned, "that instilled in me is that it's very much the quality of the teachers you have in life, the way teachers communicate with students like the way leaders communicate with employees." Another leader, Raghav, couldn't recall particular teachers but emphasized that some teachers' behaviors during his education proved great leadership examples in terms of caring for others. He recalled:

> I have quite a lot of teachers influenced me…. and it largely comes from just a passion for the subject … the passion for the subject but the ability to convey that education to the class because I really care … you know other teachers that teach and I know teachers that really powerfully educate and I come to a place of caring… now you want your clothes to be while he's just you really care that goes the extra mile you can feel it … again that's an example leadership because it talks about the place you come from…

This finding supports previous research, which states that individuals' experience of interaction with notable people subconsciously affects their relations with other people [28, 29].

The Effective Teacher's Styles—Authoritative Leadership Style

Some leaders had teachers who positively influenced their leadership styles. For example, Paul H mentioned a particular economic teacher who instilled in him values on planning and being prepared that reinforced the experience in the childhood. Paul H said, "I had a very good economics teacher… He always insisted that we all developed plans, he said you can't live unless you plan, so you must develop plans." It is similar to Angela's experience, where the teacher showed her a good example of always guiding people in a better way. Angela recalled the story about one of her teachers:

> My god father was the deputy head. A funny story was, teaching people accountability. Strict school that I went to. So uniform was quite important. He used to keep a box of very bright awful tie in his office. Everybody forgot their ties and they could not find it, he said, "no worry, I loan you one, come to my office, I lend you one." He gave them the brightest awful tie and they never forget the tie again (excited and laugh…). So little stories like that stick with me. They didn't get punishment but they didn't get what they want so they didn't forget again. I just think there is always way I mean, it does not need always about punishment and rules, we need to guide people in a better way

The reason why two teachers strongly influenced the leadership behaviors of the two leaders can be explained by their *authoritative* leadership styles. Baumrind [30] suggested that, "authoritative style is characterized by behavioural principles, high expectations of appropriate behaviour, clear statements about why certain behaviours are acceptable and others not acceptable, and warm student-teacher relationships." A study of Chamundeswari [31] with 90 female teachers and 900 students showed that the authoritative style can "yield maximum influence on academic performance among the students, followed by leadership development" due to the demand for discipline and strictness.

The present study provides evidence to support the previous finding on authoritative styles of teachers positively influencing leadership development. Paul H shared that planning was a crucial part in his journey till date. Angela also shared her passion for guiding people in doing the right things was influenced by her teacher in school. Although two leaders mentioned male teachers but support the study of Chamundeswari [31], which studied female teachers. This indicates the importance of teachers' style over teachers' gender and that authoritative is an effective teacher style (Figure 5.5).

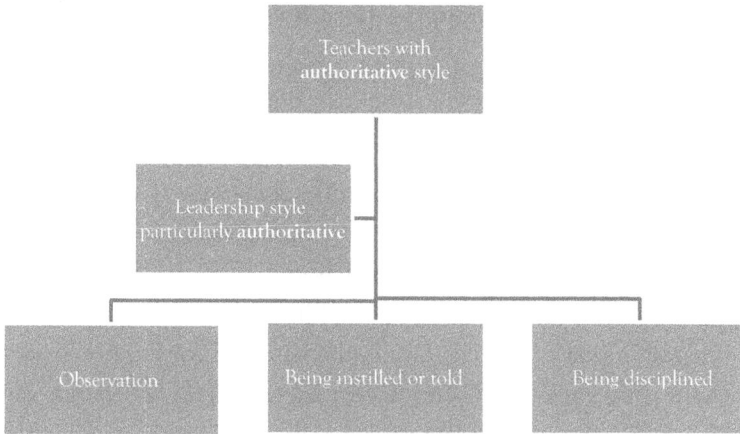

Figure 5.5 The influence process of teachers

Role Models

Everyone in society should be a role model, not only for their own self-respect, but for respect from others.

—Barry Bonds

This study illustrates that role models are significant influences on leadership development, and bad role models have a stronger influence compared to good role models, which challenges the dominant romanticizing leadership view in literature.

Ineffective Leadership Behaviors—Bad Role Models

Bad leaders' behaviors found in this study reflect toxic destructive leadership behaviors, such as one-way communication [32] or disregarding the views and long-term welfare of others [33, 34, 35]. These destructive behaviors cause uncomfortable feelings for followers because they conflict with followers' identities (identity at work theory: [36]). Such findings are consistent with previous findings emphasizing the negative impact of toxic destructive leadership (e.g., [34, 37]). However, the negative experience caused by these behaviors seems to bring positive outcomes by showing leaders how not to behave to avoid unwanted results arising from these behaviors.

Effective Leadership Behaviors—Good Role Models

Leaders in this study learned how to behave from servant and friendship leadership's behaviors, especially good listening and communication skills because these behaviors bring good results somewhat measured by their engagement at work, due to their identities recognized (identity at work theory: [36]. Such findings echo the friendship and servant leadership studies on their positive impact on followers. Servant leadership primarily aims to meet the followers' needs and interests [38], which is similar to friendship leadership [39]. Hence, the virtues of friendship provide a friendly atmosphere for leadership best exercised [40]. Friendship also reflects informality and is relational rather than positional leadership that resonates with the flexibility, informality, and unstructured of social networks. Such findings, hence, suggest the possibility of developing leadership as servant leadership and friendship, emphasizing listening and communication skills to gain effectiveness in organizational leadership and management or social networks to empower individuals (Figure 5.6).

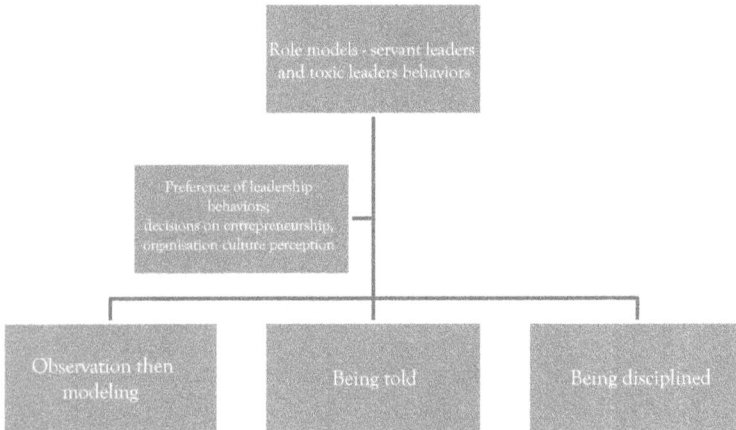

Figure 5.6 The influence process of role models

Role Model, Emotions, and Entrepreneurship Decisions

Although the influences of bad role models are not clearly stronger than good role models regarding leaders' approach toward leadership behaviors, the influence is more significant regarding leaders' new venture creation decisions. The significance is rooted in the significant emotional experiences. Emotions allow individuals to find meaning from their experiences, and then identify development transitions to adapt to the situation or environment [41, 42]. According to social identity at work, negative emotions exhibit the conflict of individuals' identity with the environment that lead to their decisions on changing the environment to protect their identity [36]. In contrast, individuals tend to engage more at work when their identities are recognized. Hence, more leaders in this study decided to quit their jobs to start their own businesses because their bad role models created negative emotional experiences to them.

Such findings partially support previous findings that entrepreneurs enter the arena to outdo their bosses (Vesper 1990) or because they dislike their bosses [6, 43]. However, this study provides deeper insights on the emotional aspects caused by negative role models, leading to new venture creation decisions. It also seems that negative role models accidently create positive outcomes in showing leaders how not to behave to avoid possible results caused by these behaviors. Hence, experiencing both negative role models, leaders appreciate more positive role models. While previous studies such as Kempster and Cope [6] only emphasize negative role models, Kempster [44] emphasizes positive role models. This book suggests that more studies need to further explore the different influences of both bad and good leaders on career paths and leadership potential of different individuals in different contexts. The dominance of negative role model also challenge the long-standing romanticized leadership literature that more investigation is needed in the often overlooked dark side of leadership [45].

Role Models and Organization Culture Perception

Apart from influencing leadership behaviors and career choices of leaders, good and bad leaders indirectly influence leaders' approach toward organizational culture in their own businesses later on. Being embedded in the organizational culture led by the role leaders, leaders are influenced by the collective group identity [46], which creates their self-concept toward organizational identity. This reinforces the literature, which suggests that leaders have a huge impact on creating organizational culture [47]. This refers to how the things are done within organizations [45]. Despite the importance of organizational culture, previous studies on leadership development, especially in an entrepreneurial context (e.g., [6, 48]), neglect this aspect. Hence, this book suggests that more investigations are needed in future research. Leadership development programs could also emphasize creating supportive learning culture to maximize the learning outcomes of individuals.

Coaches and Mentors

When the student is ready, the teacher will appear.

—The Buddha

The Mentor Appears

It was the second time I was at a speaking event in the UK as the MC of the event. At the end of the event, one man came to me and said, "Hi Jen, I saw something in you and I think I could do some help." I was over the moon as it was the second week I was in the UK, and one of my goals while in the UK was to find a mentor to boost my training and writing career to the next level.

Since that day we would meet nearly every week to discuss strategies and make videos together. He became my dear mentor and friend since that day, everyday.

A mentor shows up when a mentee is ready!

The study which is the foundation of this book found that coaches/mentors have significant impact on the leadership development journey.

Mentors—The Partner in the Development Journey

All the leaders interviewed in this study mentioned the importance of mentoring (either directly from professional mentors or indirectly from their managers or even from people on the Internet) in their career development and personal development. For example, one of the interviewed leaders, Ash, shared that he had two mentors that made him successful. One mentor runs a similar business and accelerates Ash's career development, whereas the other mentor provides him psychosocial support by reinforcing his confidence. Mentors cultivate leadership in mentees [49, 50] by empowering mentees' self-esteem [51] and showing the readiness of support mentees [52]. Ash called Matt as a good leader because he "...*makes you feel good about yourself and will give real effort into the project....*" Mentors behave as leaders when they act as examples [53]. Matt set a good example of leading by doing, which was stated in Ash's definition about leaders, "*leaders lead by setting examples....they work with people not tell people to work....and make people feel excited along the way.*"

In Greek, to mentor means to think, to counsel, to remember, and to endure. Mentors are those who have more advanced experience and knowledge [54] and benefit mentees in career development and psychosocial support [55]. The roles of the mentor can be summarized through Morris Zeldtich's description (Figure 5.7):

- **Advisors**, people having career experience willing to share their knowledge
- **Supporters**, people who give emotional and moral encouragement
- **Tutors**, people who give specific feedback on one's performance
- **Sponsors**, sources of information about and aid in obtaining opportunities
- **Models**, of identity, of the kind of person one should be to be in the chosen profession.

In this study, mentors are also found as:

- **Friends,** people who have a sense of understanding and caring
- **Challengers**, people who trust in others and challenge others to excel

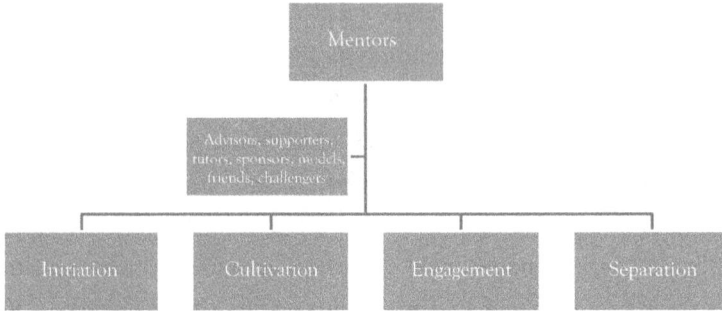

Figure 5.7 Effective mentoring process

Effective Mentoring

Mentoring generally has the following phases [7]:

- Initiation—understanding motivations for mentoring, clarity of expectation, and role
- Cultivation—setting ground rules, boundaries, goals, and criteria for success and schedule of meetings
- Engagement—focus on learning, thoughtfulness, and timely feedback
- Separation—celebrating progress, evaluation of journey together

It is recommended by the famous communication and leadership platform Toastmasters that to maximize the effectiveness program, mentors and mentees are expected to have certain attitudes as shown in Table 5.2 below:

Table 5.2 Factors ensure the effectiveness of mentoring process

Mentors	Mentees
• Available • Patient • Sensitive • Respectful • Flexible • Supportive • Knowledgeable • Confident • A good listener • Concern for others • Encouraging, Empowering, Challenging, Setting a good example	• Eager to learn • Open to new ideas • Collaborative • Grateful

Coaches

Apart from mentors, coaches were also acknowledged as important partners during the development journey of interviewed leaders.

Coaching has been defined differently in literature. According to Gil and Carrillo [56], coaching is a process that equips individuals with the tools and knowledge to develop their professionalism and increase their effectiveness [57]. In contrast, Kampa-Kokesch and Anderson [58] define coaching as a form of systematic feedback intervention to enhance professional skills, interpersonal awareness, and personal effectiveness. However, Palacios and Lumbreras [59] identify coaching as a structured and continuously monitored improvement process that helps to optimize an individual's performance [57].

Despite these various definitions, most researchers consider coaching involves a coach and a coachee and it aims to boost individual productivity and performance [57, 60] (Figure 5.8).

Effective Coaching

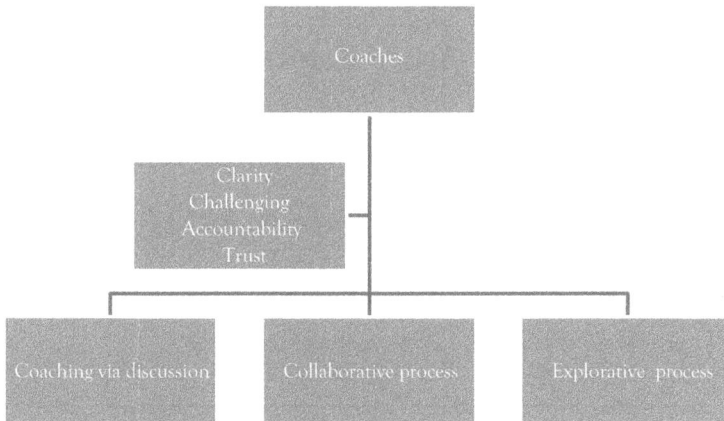

Figure 5.8 The influence process of coaching

This study found that, first, coaches help individuals to have greater understanding of themselves and their positions in their life stages. Second, coaches prepare participants for accountability in congruence with the values inculcate. Coaches guide when participants face challenges. Third, coaches challenge participants to improve everyday. Fourth, coaches help cheer up participants, be a dear friend during their development journey, and trust their leadership and their goals.

Reflection Corner

How to find a mentor or coach:
- *Go to Google and search for the nearest coaches and book their free sessions* (I also provide free coaching or mentoring section at jenvuhuong.com /resultscoaching)
- *Try various coaches and choose one that you feel you can work with*
- *Try to be a coach for someone else, just listen*
- *Be your own mentor, think about your future self and what your future self will suggest you*

You always have at least one mentor/coach—yourself! Coaching can be also done by individuals themselves, which is called "self-coaching" [61, 62, 63].

Self-coaching is a process of guiding individual growth and development [64]. The effectiveness of self-coaching principally depends on leaders' self-management skills [63]. Self-coaching strengthens self-management skills [61, 62], which can lead to higher productivity [65].

Action Corner

Filling out the following incomplete sentences as a foundation for you to take action based on the findings of the study about mentoring/coaching

Three mentors/coaches helping me to move to the next level in life are…

I will go to go to find my mentor/coach on….

The persons for who I can be a mentor/coach are…

Community-Based Networks

Every successful individual knows that his or her achievement depends on a community of persons working together.

—Paul Ryan

Creating a Network Is the Leadership Itself

Nobody was willing to help me, I was on my own. When I was doing this 30 years ago there were no networking groups, there was no mentors, none of the support groups that there are now. One of the reasons why I run the meet-up for entrepreneurs, because I know it is so nice to come to someone sometimes and say, "oh my God this is happening," or even just talk to someone, and discover they're going through the same thing as other people, I know how that can get quite lonely.

Inside the community, when we have the meetings, it's not always about me, it's about them. Even if I'm running the meeting, I'll try to get everyone to speak, even people who don't like speaking. I bring balloons, and if you catch the balloon you need to introduce yourself, or I will have games of bingo, so you have to go and find people that for example speak French, or are plumbers, you have to fill the card out. So it means you have to go and speak to other people. If we have a topic, I might have someone come and talk to the group, but I then encourage the group to talk about the experience, or what are they looking for. It is encouraging everyone to join and support each other; it's not about just one person or just me.

This is what Carolyn, the organizer of one of the most popular business meetups in Bristol, shared about how she started her own community-based network:

Creating a network even can start with a simple idea. Another leader, Jo, shared:

Christmas Day with my kids … I think whether 'are there any positive people in Bristol' and it was just that how it started and that's why the group ended up called positive people. So I on that day I set out the group on my app on the run on a holiday and then by the time I got home we don't like 50 people join, I was like … but yes which is great and there are definitely positive people in Bristol.

Community and Entrepreneurial Leadership Development

This study provides evidence that involving or creating community-based social networks of people having the same interests or needs, greatly influences leader's entrepreneurial leadership development (Figure 5.9).

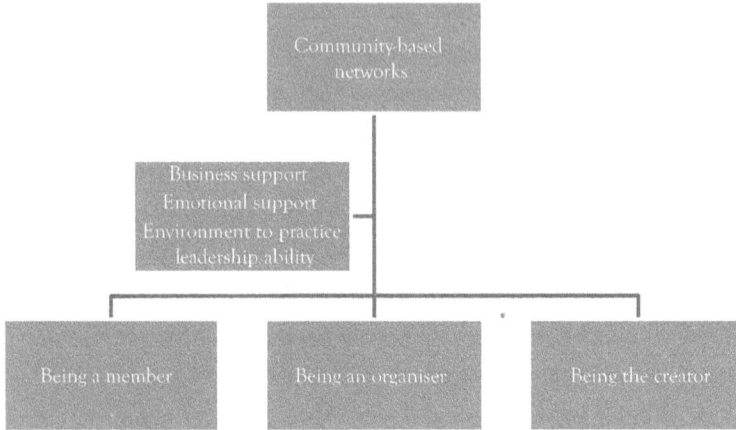

Figure 5.9 The influence process of community-based networks

In particular, social networks helped the interviewed leaders gain business support (information, advice, opportunity, reputation) and emotional support (confidence, accountability). These were and are important for them to lead their businesses. It is suggested that entrepreneurs are naturally embedded in social networks, and they need to find resources such as skills, labor, and motivation to start and maintain their businesses [66, 67]. The rich, socially embedded experiences of different individuals in social networks [68] become sources of information, advice, contacts, and reputation for entrepreneurs [66]. Social networks based on a community can also create a sense of community where individuals share certain values [69] that provide emotional support and accountability for individuals.

Such findings in this study are also consistent with previous research on entrepreneurial leadership, which emphasizes similar contributions of social networks to the entrepreneurial process (e.g., [6, 67, 70, 71, 72]). Moreover, the creation of social networks of female leaders in this study illustrates that social networks are results of leadership development overtime and provide the environment to reinforce leadership identity. This reinforces the statement by Cullen-Lester et al. [73] that social networks are leadership development outcomes as social networks that gather individuals and create resource mobilization and exchange that help individuals achieve their goals [74].

Despite the positive impact of social networks, most leadership development research and programs emphasize formal contexts [73]. The flexibility, flat structure, and relational leadership in community-based social networks [75] provide entrepreneurs the flexibility and autonomy, which are often the motivation for entrepreneurs to start businesses [76]. This may enhance their engagement in learning through social networks rather than through formal training. Moreover, it seems that learning from liked-minded people, especially other entrepreneurs, is more time-saving and practical than from formal training classrooms. Hence, this study contributes to most recent research (e.g., [6, 73, 77]) that emphasize incorporating social networks in leadership development programs, especially for SMEs leaders.

However, apart from the dominant positive sides of social networks, this study provides evidence that social networks can negatively influence leadership identity such as creating problems of multiple identities, as in the case of Darren, who is perceived differently outside and inside his network. Recently, Ford [78] and Ford et al. [79] also stated that individual leaders pose multiple competing identities due to social preference that can lead to anxiety and inauthenticity. This can be explained by the fact that social networks may create collective group identity, which influences how each individual perceives other individual's identity [46]. It seems that the interviewed leaders in this study have certain tolerance to the negative side of social networks that may explain their emphasis on positive impacts of social networks.

It is suggested that negative ties may impact human behaviors by reinforcing positive ties [80, 81]. However, most researchers focus on the positive side of social networks on leadership development (e.g., [6, 73, 77]) [82]. Recently, Chiu et al. [82] suggested that leaders who are central to social networks are perceived positively by their followers compared with those who avoid their social networks. Therefore, these study findings suggest scope for future research to discover both sides of social networks on leadership development to develop a clearer picture for leadership development programs incorporating social networks.

Reflection Corner

The ladder of effective networking comes from being a member in a community till being a community creator.

- *Find a network that you are interested in based on your interests/hobbies (and even you are not interested in businesses, it is still useful to schedule your time to go to at least one business meeting per week because business people are really dynamic and proactive and have positive energy).*
- *In each meeting, choose at least 3 people you think that can help you to move forward and schedule meetings with them.*
- *Keeping in touch with people.*
- ***The winning mindset—giving***
  We often fall into the trap of thinking that wealthy and successful people already have everything and they do not need anything from you. This mindset accidentally makes you underestimate your values as well as the bigger picture. Change the way of thinking and ask yourself, "what can I bring into this relationship?" Think about any contacts as people not positions.
- *Be the listener: this is a golden rule when communicating with people. Be genuinely interested in others is the key of connection. Make sure in one meeting, you listen more than speak if you want to understand about the person you speak with. For more detailed on communication, the book 'how to win friends and influence people' is a great reference.*

There are different networks that you can go to: Toastmasters, Meetup, Networking group on Facebook, Internationals, Embassy.

And one more important choice: If you don't find it, create one!

Action Corner

Filling out the following incomplete sentences as a foundation for you to take action based on the findings of the study about community-based social networks:

A network event that I will attend this week is…

A network that I can create now to share values is…

Three main values that can add to others through networking are…

Psychological Factors

Self-Learning Driven/Curiosity

You learn not because you have to. But because it is who you are.

—Inhisthoughts

Be a Massive Advocate for Learning

"I used all the money of training course to buy books." This statement of an interviewed leader, Craig, stuck in my head. Craig shared how his drive to learn:

> I went on a training course—Certified Scrum Master and Certified Scrum Product Owner…one went well and the other didn't very well ….And the reason left halfway through the course because I didn't get any value from the course basically… I ended up getting refunded for the course because the trainer was wasn't I wasn't great and the company refunded me of course… I agreed with my boss——the head of operations that I would spend that money on reading tools…So I went on to buy four hundreds of pounds worth of books and in further going on the training course, I got a library of information that I then liked…

Similar to Craig, Jo emphasized the importance of self-learning:

> I'm a massive advocate for learning… I was just like a sponge, I just loved the books… I nag all of my clients to read, learn, watch, listen—because that what has made me successful over the years… I was a head chef…I didn't have any leadership skills at that point. But luckily because I was reading personal development books, I started to develop the skills I needed…All other interviewed leaders also acknowledged self-learning as their key driver during their entrepreneurial journey which echoes the importance of learning in leadership development.

Self-Learning—The Vehicle of the Development Process

The interviewed leaders come from different backgrounds, some of them studied A level, some studied master's, some studied PhD, but some even did not finish high schools. However, all of them educated themselves through self-learning.

Self-learning (or autodidacticism) is education without the guidance of masters (such as teachers and professors) or institutions (such as schools). Self-learning is considered the modern form of learning that somehow replaces traditional, instructional learning. Self-directed learning has been proven to be effective, convenient, and fast, thanks to the rise of the Internet.

Learning on our own can also help us explore different ways of thinking, and we can go through difficult concepts on our own without help. Hence, self-learning helps us develop the confidence we need to tackle challenging problems and obstacles in life.

A recent qualitative study of Sun et al. [83] suggests that student's **self-efficacy** in learning math and the use of help-seeking strategies are all significantly positively related with academic achievement in both pre- and in-class learning environments.

The research which this book is based on also found the importance of self-learning in excelling the performance of interviewed leaders. As most these entrepreneurs do not attend formal training programs, understanding sources for their self-learning process is important.

Sources for Self-Learning

There are three major sources of learning found in this study: books, podcasts, aesthetic materials such as TED talks and novels. Various benefits were highlighted using these materials for self-learning purpose. The following table gives some examples of the various good self-learning sources (check the full list at jenvuhuong.com/modelsuccess) (Table 5.3).

Each of us may prefer different ways of learning. There would be no right or wrong way. Some business owners who were interviewed shared that they did not read many books but they watched a lot of videos or listened to podcasts, they are successful. Some use people as the main source of learning, learning from every single person they met in life. The most important thing is the drive of learning—NONSTOP, despite ages.

Table 5.3 Resources for self-learning

Sources	Category	Books	Authors
	Self-development books	*Think and Grow rich*	Napoleon Hill
		I can do it	Louise Hay
		How to Win Friends and Influence People	Dale Carnegie
		Awaken the Giant Within	Tony Robbins
		Motivation manifesto	Brendon Burchard
	Business books	*The high performance habits*	Brendon Burchard
		Money master of the games	Tony Robbins
		Principles	Ray Dalio
		Crush It	Gary Vaynerchuk
	Biography of successful people	*Dreams from My Father*	Barack Obama
		Long Walk to Freedom	Nelson Mandela
	Novels	*Sherlock Holmes*	Conan Doyle
		As a Man Thinketh	James Allen
		The Alchemist	Paulo Coelho
Podcasts	Self-development and business development	*Live an extraordinary life*	The Tony Robbins Podcast
		The charged life	The Brendon show
		Self-mastery	The Robin Sharma Mastery Sessions
		Inspiring stories of brilliant business minds, world-class athletes and influential celebrities	The school of Greatness with Lewis The impact Theory with Tim Bilyeu The Tim Ferriss Show
	Business	*Innovation, leadership, and change in the world of leadership*	Innovation Ecosystem with Mark Bidwell
Ted talks or YouTube channels	Ted talks	*Draw your future—Take control of your life*	Patti Dobrowolski
		How great leaders inspire action	Simon Sinek
		Inside the mind of a master procrastinator	Tim Urban
		How to stop screwing yourself over	Mel Robbins
		Why we do what we do	Tony Robbins
		Stanford Commencement Address	Steve Jobs
	YouTube channels	Similar to podcast channels	

No matter what is the source of your learning, I believe the most important thing is to learn and then test it out then optimize it.

Effective Self-Learning

Here are some tips for self-learning effectively through reading:

- Make a list of books that we want to read, following either categories or authors (Figure 5.10)
- Schedule: Using 5W rule—When (date and time), Where, What to read, Which way (e-books or printed books), for What purpose
- Use a pencil to write or mark some important information when reading (if you use printed books)
- Use a notebook to summarize main ideas:
  - Lesson learned or interesting ideas
  - What to share with others
  - What to implement right away
- Do reflection to take action

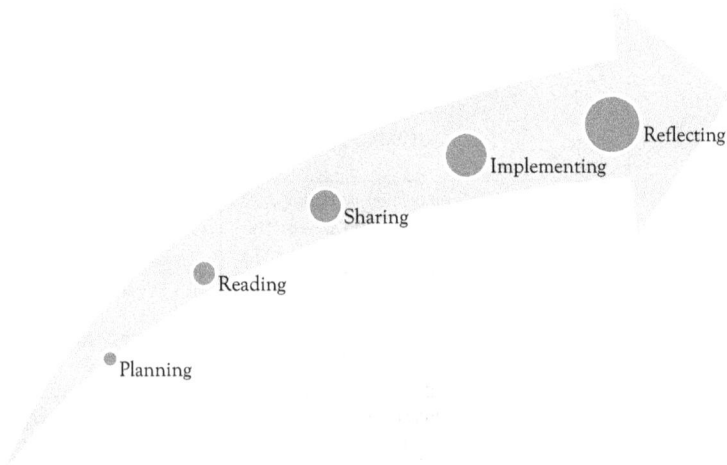

Figure 5.10 Effective reading process

The question of how to read effectively also leads to the question of how to increase the reading speed. For this topic, the best-selling author Tim Ferries should be given credits.

I found that the two following techniques shared by Tim are quite effective:

- Technique 1:
    - Use a pencil to track your progress. Underline each line when reading, focus on the tip of the pencil, and read following its direction. Do not worry about comprehension (because you are learning to increase your speed reading).
    - Each line reads in 1s, only 1s.
    - Then switch to the next line and then the next page.
    - You need to follow the 1s rule. Maybe at first you are not familiar and do not know all the content of the paragraph you read, but as with other muscles in your body, by using more of your brain the speed of your reading increases and you gain more focus. Enough to understand the main idea of the content you read.

(Do this for three minutes, take a break and then repeat the exercise)

- Technique 2:
    - Ignore some words on the sides of the book you read, and only read those words in the middle of the page.
    - Imagine if each of the lines has 10 words, by reducing the number of words read by three or four letters on a line, you only need to read 6/7 letters on each line; if a page has 20 lines, you only need to read 120 to 140 words instead of 200!
    - Just like with our first technique, at first you may not understand much of the content but as your brain muscles get better and more focused, you will grasp more and more from the main idea.

Reflection Corner

You can easily find the list of these books/podcasts/Ted talks on the Internet, but there is one source that is much more difficult to find and I believe we don't read from it often enough—the book inside us. It would be much more difficult for some of us to be quite and read our thoughts and our ideas. We are often in a rush and are easily caught up by the busy schedule in everyday life. If we can schedule time to read books of others, we also need to schedule time to read our own "book" for at least a few minutes per day and longer once a week.

We cannot deny the benefits of reading books of others as we can obtain the knowledge/tools of people in years of experiencing in their life just in some hours. However, the possible ineffective side of it is that we may try to be someone like people in the books instead of using what we learn to be our better self.

You may also ask "what is the best source of learning?" The answer is inside you. You need to do more critical reflection on your thinking and behaviors as well as sometimes practice asking yourself questions to critically think to solve problems and create new things.

Action Corner

Filling out the following incomplete sentences as a foundation for you to take action based on the findings of the study about self-learning:

- *The list of books I will read this year, three months, one month, one week, one day*

- *The list of books I will read this month …*

- *The list of videos I will watch this month …*

- *…*

- *The three things that I will learn this month…*

- *The three things I will learn today …*

- *The three things I learn from my old experience….*

Experimentation/Trial and Error—The Practitioner for the Development Journey

Evening is a time of real experimentation. You never want to look the same way.

—Donna Karan

It was trial and error…

It was trial and error, it was doing things and reflecting on things, so it might be setting up a group, bringing people in… it might be working with young offender and if it went well why did it go well or that went horribly wrong what would I do different

James shared about how he learned his leadership through experimenting.

All leaders acknowledge the important of experimentation in validating their learning. Experimentation helps individuals validate their learning not only through self-learning but also from previous experiences in the employed context and critical reflection helps them to increase their self-awareness of what to include and not include to further their development process [84, 85], which reflects an effective leadership development [6, 86].

Self-Reflection—The Adjustment of the Development of the Journey

Follow effective action with quiet reflection. From the quiet reflection, will come even more effective action.

—Peter Drucker

My Sister's Diary

When I was a kid, I often saw my sister writing her diary. I became curious and one day I secretly read her diary (which is not a recommended behavior). I began understanding her more. I could see how difficult she had to experience. Since then I learned to do self-reflection by writing and it made me read my own mind/behaviors moment by moment. It became a great weapon of increasing self-awareness and slowing down.

Reflection—The Adjustment of the Journey

All leaders reflected that reflection is a big part of their development process to unlearn what are not good and what are good. "It's a way of being…you cannot know how to do differently without reflecting on what you have done…It can be a journaling time or every moment," Poku, shared.

According to *Cambridge Dictionary*, self-reflection is the activity of thinking about your own feelings and behavior, and the reasons that may lie behind them. Critical reflection [86] is considered relevant with regard to entrepreneurial leadership development [6] by increasing the self-awareness of individuals [85]. Through critical reflection, leaders make sense of what is relevant for them [87].

Research by Giada Di Stefano, Francesca Gino, Gary Pisano, and Bradley Staats in call centers demonstrated that employees who spent 15 minutes at the end of the day reflecting about lessons learned performed 23 percent better after 10 days than those who did not reflect. A study of UK commuters found a similar result when those who were prompted to use their commute to think about and plan for their day were happier, more productive, and less burned out than people who didn't.

According to a *Havard Business Review* expert, there are a few main reasons why people don't do self-reflection: (i) Don't understand the process; (ii) Don't like the process (slow down, adopt a mindset of not knowing and curiosity, tolerate messiness and inefficiency, and take personal responsibility); (iii) Don't like the results (dismiss the noted strengths and dislike the noted weaknesses); (iv) Have a bias toward action (Reflection can feel like staying in the center of the goal and missing the action); (v) Can't see a good Return of Investment.

Effective Self-Reflection?

We need to get some aside time for self-reflection—yearly, monthly, weekly, and daily. Every evening can be a good time to reflect upon what we have gone through during the day; weekend can be a good time to reflect upon the whole week. However, the most suitable time as well as the frequency of doing reflection also depends on each individual, so individuals need to test by themselves.

Porter, one of the well-known executive coaches, shared that the most difficult clients according to her are people who don't reflect especially on themselves. Here is one of her suggestion for self-reflection:

- **Select a reflection process that matches your preferences**: You can sit, walk, bike, or stand, alone or with a partner, writing, talking, or thinking.
- **Schedule time:** Schedule your reflection time and then commit to keep it. And if you find yourself trying to skip it or avoid it, reflect on that!
- **Identify some important questions**
  - What are you avoiding?
  - How are you helping your colleagues achieve their goals?
  - How are you not helping or even hindering their progress?
  - How might you be contributing to your least enjoyable relationship at work?
  - How could you have been more effective in a recent meeting?
- **Start small**: If an hour of reflection seems like too much, try 10 minutes. Set yourself up to make progress, even if it feels small.
- There are some questions to ask when doing self-reflection:
  1. Am I living up to my core values and personal mission?
  2. Am I being a person others can respect?
  3. Am I respecting my body the way I should?
  4. Am I meeting the expectations I set for others around me?
  5. Am I using my talents fully?
  6. Am I performing at my peak capacity?
  7. Am I giving my family and friends my most and my best?
  8. Am I engaging in a worthy activity?
  9. Am I making a positive impact on the world?
  10. Am I on the path to my preferred future?

(Visit Jenvuhuong.com/reflection for more detailed information)

Reflection Corner

One day you wake up in the morning and you hear somebody knocking the door. You open the door, suddenly you see your future self, standing there, healthy, wealthy and tell you that they want you to do something differently. Write down all the possible things that the future you tell you to do differently and take action upon that.

Action Corner

Filling out the following incomplete sentences as a foundation for you to take action based on the findings of the study about reflection:

Three things that I feel thankful for today are...

Three things I learned today are...

Three things I can do better are...

Purpose—The Drive of the Development Journey

The heart of human excellence often begins to beat when you discover a pursuit that absorbs you, frees you, challenges you, or gives you a sense of meaning, joy, or passion.

—Terry Orlick

The Man Follows His Calling

I learned that traveling and moving around the country, and having a good time didn't fulfill something in me, that I had some missing pieces that needed to be fulfilled. I felt like I needed to fulfill something in me, the desire to make myself better. I knew I had skills to help other people make their lives better. There is a child's story where a person learns skills and then goes traveling to speak to a wise monk, and then returns back to his homeland to help people. Maybe that's what happened (smile). I had a calling to go back my own hometown...

Ben, shared the calling in coming to contribute for his hometown after living in different places.

Purpose—The Drive of the Development Journey

Most leaders in the study mentioned that their leadership development journey is linked with having a sense of purpose/calling. Interestingly, the older leaders get, the stronger they felt toward the need for having a sense of purpose. It can be explained that they tend to focus on the need of certainty—safety, money, survival—at their early age.

Several researchers also refer to leadership as a purpose (e.g., [88]). These researchers clarify their argument, "Many commentators (e.g., [89, 90]) argue that leadership is entwined with notions of vision, mission, shared goals, objectives and plans. Such notions emphasize the importance of leadership oriented toward enabling the achievement of something significant. In a sense they are all in some way implicitly associated with purpose."

Practically, according to the survey, 90 percent of people who worked in a purpose-driven organization reported feeling engaged in their work. In companies that aren't as focused on purpose, only 32 percent of employees reported feelings of engagement and connectedness with the work they were doing [91]. Studies also show that companies with teams focused on their organization's purpose had annual growth rates nearly three times the annual rate for their entire industry [91].

Purpose—The Sense of Growth and Contribution

Most of the leaders referred purpose with a meaningful feeling associated with personal growth or contribution to family or society. In their words, the sense of purpose is supporting the family, making a difference, freedom, learning, be their best, leading, and help others.

Having a purpose helps the interviewed leaders in different aspects: stay focused, feel passionate about your goal, increase clarity, feel gratified, live a value-based life.

How to Have a Sense of Purpose

Defining life purpose traps a lot of us into thinking that life's purpose is something huge or ambiguous or just only for some particular talented people. The fact is that the sense of purpose comes from how do we perceive what we do more than what we do. The sense of purpose comes, first, from acknowledging our personal values.

Therefore, we can choose to make a powerful meaning of our values and choose to take action on it to enhance our values over time. The action can start with learning everything everyday to increase the personal values and contribute to life. Contribution can start with small little things such as being nice and kind to others. It comes from the intention of kindness, care, and love (Figure 5.11).

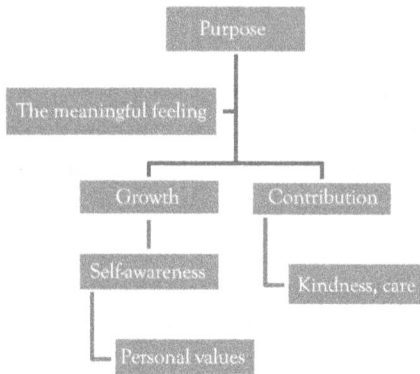

Figure 5.11 Process to live on purpose

Reflection Corner

In February 2015, I went bankrupt financially and mentally after quitting my engineering consultant job. Each morning I woke up, having the pressure of how to survive in the next days, I still strongly felt there was something important waiting for me ahead. I felt that strongly and I knew I would figure things out. Despite having nothing to eat, I still wrote everyday, I lived everyday. Thanks to the power of having a purpose, I figured the way out to finally work full-time in what I love to do.

That sense of purpose of doing something bigger than yourself help us to be bigger than any situation to overcome difficulties.

Having a sense of purpose, we are always being pulled forward without necessarily pushing ourselves.

Action Corner

Filling out the following incomplete sentences as a foundation for you to take action based on the findings of the study about purpose:

- *Meaning: Things makes me feel meaningful when I do?*

- *Growth: what helps me grow everyday?*

- *Lifetime: what I still feel doing in the next five years?*

- *Contribution: what do I want to contribute to life?*

> *By asking the preceding questions, you may define your purpose, if you still feel not clear, let self-development, love and kindness be your everyday purpose. When you are developed, the big picture will be clearer. The most important thing is to know the big picture is always there and live everyday on the purpose of developing you and be nice to others.*

Decision—The Starting Point of a New Development Chapter

It is in your moments of decision that your destiny is shaped.
— Tony Robbins

The Turning Point

> *There was also was an incident, something that did hit me. Again when I was only 25 or 26 I was working in a company in London and the offices were based in an old merchant's house, six floors with a big staircase going up in the middle. It was about 6 o'clock in the evening when we heard someone outside our office, we heard a woman sort of crying, like a gasp or scream… It was a complete shock to me, my first reaction was to wait for someone else to help, when is something happens you think someone else is going to help, but they don't. So someone eventually steps forward and I was that someone. It was a big turning point in my life, I got these 50-year-olds to do what I told them to do, I got my bosses running around doing what I told them to do.*

Carolyn shared her experience that changed her whole life journey— making a decision to take up leadership role in any situation and taking responsibility.

Decisions—The Starting Point of a New Development Chapter

Leaders in this study confirmed that their journey is moved to a new chapter by decisions. There are two different TRIGGERS that help leaders

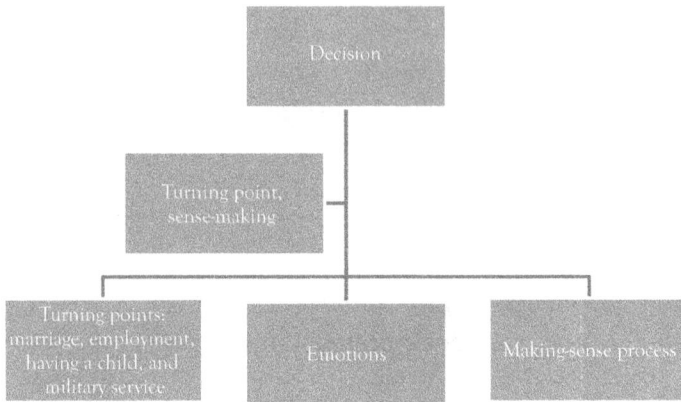

Figure 5.12 Decision making process

make their decisions to take ownership of the situation or their life or change jobs that influenced their leadership development (Figure 5.12):

- Being under a pressure that hurts their identity/their personal values or experiencing a moral situation—seeing others suffer by something or someone
- Being inspired or motivated by someone or somebody or an event

All the events or moments only lead to a decision through the sense-making process of an individual. Hence, having an empowering sense-making process of disempowering sense-making process will influence the quality of decisions that individuals make.

The decision is made at a turning point during their development journey. According to the life course approach (e.g., [92, 93]), turning points can come from single dramatic events that embrace abrupt changes or occur gradually over time to the point an "epiphany" triggers a decision to radically change one's life. Some common turning points in the life course of an individual are marriage, employment, having a child, and military service.

During these turning points, individuals make sense of the events and make a decision to change their life trajectory. Day et al. [94] cite "one central challenge facing scientific psychology is the development of comprehensive accounts of why humans progress along different life trajectories" [95] to emphasize the importance of understanding how individuals progress during their life trajectories as leaders. Little evidence found in discovering the making sense process and the interrelationship of leadership development and turning points. Harms et al. [96] suggests that developmental trajectories influence on the rate of leader development. A recent study suggests that experiencing conflict between personal and professional identities, manifested through different socialization experiences over time, can lead to a "turning point" and a decision that affects a person's career trajectory of 17 male and female the academic who becomes Head of Department in a post-1992 UK university [97].

Individuals make sense of their turning points to make decisions. In particular, emotions allow individuals to make meaning of the experiences, then identify the development transitions [98, 99] to adapt to the contexts or environment [41, 100, 101, 102]. Individuals tend to make decisions to change based on the significance of the emotions, not the positive or negative aspects of emotions [103]. The more the conflict of different contextual factors (e.g., the past and the current event), the more the likelihood that individuals experience strong emotions, leading them to make changes to adapt [104, 105].

This study provides evidence in the influence of turning points either from single dramatic events (e.g., losing a family member, having cancer, or having a child) or from events accumulated overtime (e.g., long time of being depressed). The study gives evidence that turning points of leaders' related emotions that are either negative (e.g., being bullied by bad leaders) or positive emotions (e.g., having a child) but both provoke leaders to make a change.

This indicates the importance of examining the turning points and development trajectory, as Day et al. [94] suggests after reviewing 25 years' leadership research. Moreover, it suggests an indication for leadership training program in creating a mindset shift through provoking emotional aspects instead of solely focusing on skills and competencies.

Based on this flow (Figure 5.13), we can either influence on the events, emotions or make sense to make a good decision.

How to Make a Good Decision

Lacking the ability to make good decisions is a major reason for procrastination as well as failure. Decisions help us save time and make better use of resources, having a stronger commitment, and avoid procrastination. There are different ways of defining decision: (i) the ability to decide

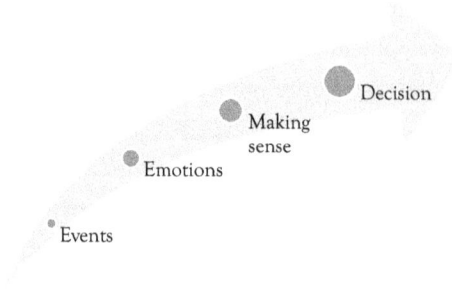

Figure 5.13 Decision making process based on an event

quickly and without pausing because you are not certain and (ii) a choice that you make about something after thinking about several possibilities.

Regardless of the definition of decision, decisions impact behaviors, results, and then the person's quality of life. Our life is a continuity of different decisions, ranging from small ones such as what to eat to the big ones like where to live. The quality of decisions (both consciously or unconsciously) decide the quality of our life. However, not all of us have skills to make a good decision.

To answer the question of how to make a good decision, the answers will be varied for different situations. There are some decisions that we don't have time to think about, there are some decisions we have longer time to think about. Despite the contextual dependence, there are four fundamental elements of a good decision:

- Making a decision in a good state of mind
- Sooner is better
- Stick to it
- Fully take responsibility

Decision making is like a muscle that we can learn to train it for stronger everyday.

Prepare a Really Good State of Mind

No effective decision is made in a bad mood or bad state of mind. We need to put ourselves into a good state of mind before making a decision. We can go for a small walk or just simply do some stretching or just go for washing our faces if we are in a lousy mood.

The Sooner, The Better

Although some decisions may take longer time than others, the sooner we make a decision, the better it is. For example, if we decide to move to another country to live for a while, it may take a longer time than deciding to go to a meeting or not. No matter what, over analyzing paralyzing often leads to procrastination. Making quick definite decisions is the antidote for procrastination. Hence, we can refer to other following points to make decisions sooner.

Make a Decision and Stick to it

Sometimes the decisions make us feel fearful because of the changes we need to make, even though we know if we make them happen, the results would be good; we should make the decisions and stick to them.

Instead of wondering and being worried, we should make the decisions sooner.

Stop putting it off, make that decision and, most importantly, stick to it.

Take Full Responsibility for the Decision Made

Once a decision is made, we need to take full responsibility for whatever happens later on.

Reflection Corner

It was dark. It was quiet. There was nobody on the road at that late hour in my little village. My mum had punished me by leaving me outside on a dark road because I hadn't done my homework.

I was five years old. I didn't cry. I didn't scream. I stood there, and I felt bitter. I asked myself why I had made my mum punish me; it was because I didn't do something that would benefit my life. I asked myself why I let my mum remind me that I needed to take responsibility for my life.

My mum got a bit worried so she took me back inside after a few minutes. She was surprised to see me not crying, not resisting. She did not see that her child had made a decision to change her whole life later by "fully taking responsibility for her life to not let her mum worry about her anymore." My mum didn't know a stubborn kid had been shaped inside me at that very moment.

I had made a decision. I decided to live such a life that nobody would have to worry about me. I decided to take ownership of my life. I became aware that nobody was going to take care of my life better than I was. Who could take ownership of a person better than the person herself or himself? Nobody. I decided to be stubborn in my decision. This decision made my life.

Action Corner

Filling out the following incomplete sentences below as a foundation for you to take action based on the findings of the study about decision:

The decision I need to make now to change my life for better is…

To stick with the decisions, I need to do three things…

Context Factors

This study found that leadership development journey depends on different contexts, similarly to the model of Jepson: (i) the immediate social (SMEs), (ii) the general cultural (British, European, American, Asian), and (iii) the historical or institutional context (experiencing in both being employed and running businesses) (Figure 5.14).

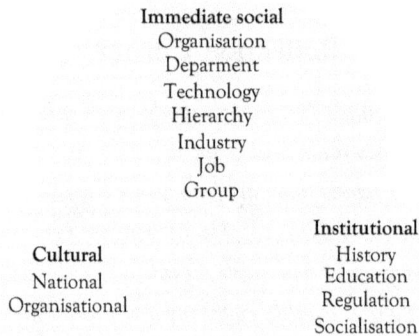

Immediate social
Organisation
Deparment
Technology
Hierarchy
Industry
Job
Group

Institutional
History
Education
Regulation
Socialisation

Cultural
National
Organisational

Figure 5.14 Context framework [106]

Leadership Development Outcomes

Leadership development outcomes are the mix of identity, perspectives, behaviors, and skills. One of the most important skills found in all narratives is listening.

All participants suggest that identity/perspective/behavior/skills/styles change overtime. The framework for change is based on the following steps: (i) identify the current patterns; (ii) identify which patterns that you want to keep or develop; (iii) make it become a daily practice (habit).

Identity Development

- Using reflection to reflect upon the patterns of your identity, how could you describe your best self in three words.
- To develop our best self, just identify three words to describe your best self. Bring these words with you and remind yourself to live up to that person every single day.

Perspective Development

- Reflect on identifying the patterns of your perspectives
- Decide which perspectives you want to reinforce
- Look at the experience from different perspectives following time or a third person

Behavioral Development

- Reflect on identifying your current patterns
- Decide which behaviors you want to reinforce

Skills Development

- Identify what skills do you need to develop to become the leader you want to be
- No matter what skills you define, one skill must be in your list—listening

Listening

You were born with two ears and one mouth for a reason.

—Epictetus

(so that we can listen twice as much as we speak)

Listening has different levels: listening to others, listening to the world, listening to one self.

Effective Listening

We can listen at about twice the speed the average person talks. That means we can speak at a rate of 125 to 150 words per minute, but we can hear, process, and analyze at a rate of 400 to 800 words per minute. The extra time between what you say and what is heard can be used positively or negatively in the communication process.

Some Keys for Listening:

- Genuinely approach everyone with curiosity to learn about them
- Empty your thoughts or assumptions to welcome sharing from others
- Ask questions
- Elaborate on what you hear and ask them to elaborate more
- Share what you feel/think

Active Listen:

- Listen and hear rather than waiting to speak.
- Watch body language.
- Find common ground.
- Paraphrase the speaker's words back to him or her as a question: "I see/hear/feel like you· are afraid of...", "It seems like she really confuses you."
- Clarifying: Bringing vague material into sharper focus "Let me see if I've got it all..."
- Perception Checking: Request for verification of your perceptions.
- "Let me see if I've got this right. You said you feel the project is important, but at the same time you find it frustrating. Is that what you are saying?"

- Validation: Acknowledge the individual's challenges and feelings.
- "I appreciate your willingness to talk about…"
- Summarizing: Pulling it all together, organizing and integrating the major aspects of your dialogue, "So it sounds to me as if…"
- Empathy: Reflection of content and feeling.
- "Your feel (state feeling) because (state content)."
- Remember that silence (as well as long pauses) can be golden.

Barriers to Active Listening:

- Distractions
- Trigger words
- Vocabulary
- Limited attention span
- Emotions
- Noise and visual distraction
- Cultural differences
- Interrupting or influencing

Strategic Listening:

- Tell me more about _____?
- How'd you get to that conclusion _____?
- O.k., what was another time when _____?
- What have you learned about _____?
- I'd be interested in knowing your reasons for _____?

Reflection corner—Let's go out for a meal together

Maryl, my close friend at university, often called me to join her for a meal at late night anytime she met any problems. Although I didn't eat, she didn't mind to have me join her as long as I would listen to her. Maryl would tell me what she though and all things happened in her daily life anytime we met.

There was no special reason why Maryl often wanted to go out with me but for listening and understanding. I didn't say anything but just listened. I could see how passionate she was to speak when having someone to listen to her passionately.

Action Corner

Filling out the following incomplete sentences as a foundation for you to take action based on the findings of the study about listening:

One person I can ask for their sharing today is…

3 ways to help me listen to others people more effectively…

3 things that I can eliminate to make my active listening more effective…

Communication

There are two differences kinds of communication: verbal and nonverbal

- Verbal: requires formal language, words, vocabulary, symbols
- Nonverbal: independent of formal language, body language, facial expressions, colors, shapes, rhythmic sounds

Nonverbal communication accounts for the majority of effective communication so you want to make nonverbal communication support for your verbal communication. To learn more tips about becoming a competent communicator you can visit jenvuhuong.com/competentspeaker

Tips for Body Language:

- Mirror the other person's body language to convey understanding
- Respect personal space: most people need a "Bubble Area," which is equal to about three feet or arm's length away from another person. The goal is to be close enough to be attentive but be far enough for comfort
- To create a positive message, think SOLER (S—Smile; O—Openness; L—Lean Forward; E—Eye contact; R—Relax)

Leadership Development Environment

This study found that friendship in collaborative environment is the best environment for developing leadership. Friendship creates a friendly environment where people with different ideas, assumptions, experiences, expectations, and ambitions can freely harmony work together (Figure 5.15).

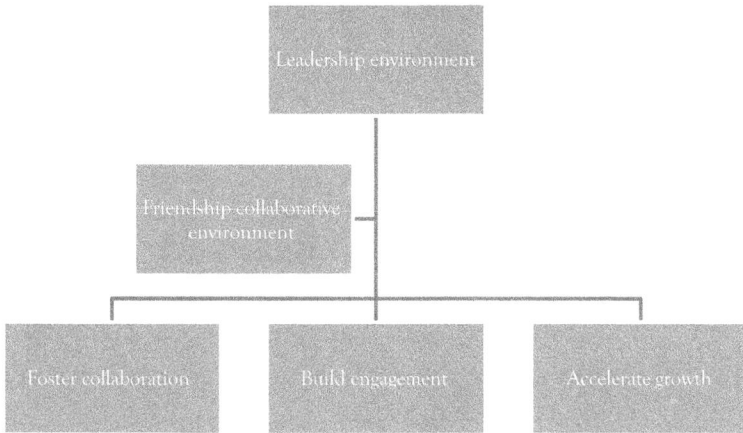

Figure 5.15 Leadership development environment

According to the interviewed leaders, friendly environment fosters collaboration between people as people consider each other as friends, so they are willing to share ideas and respect others' ideas. Moreover, friendship environment also builds engagement of employees. Some interviewed leaders suggest that they felt more satisfied in the environment where they had some good friends. Besides, good friends also challenge each other to grow.

Implications

This study suggests different practices for leadership development at four different levels: family, school, organizational, and policy levels.

Family and School Level

Leadership and parenting practices both relate to the process of influencing others to achieve desired outcomes. As leadership development starts from early childhood, parents and educators play an important role being involved in empowering leadership potential in children. In particular, parents and teachers may want to emphasize listening and communicating to understand children's interests and ultimately empower their leadership potential by giving them opportunities to lead. Parents also could be cautious in creating cultural distinction in children to avoid hindering their exposure to other cultures, entrepreneurialism, and leadership opportunities.

Besides, parents and school could encourage children to learn through reading books about successful entrepreneurs and leaders to expose them to an entrepreneurial mindset. Aesthetic and art learning materials such as Ted Talk or novels should be incorporated in learning materials to enhance children's ability of solving problems, creativity, and enact children's potential. Thanks to sport activities, children can embrace self-confidence and teamwork abilities, children should be encouraged to participate in these activities. However, it is necessary to design sports activities suitable for different levels of performance to maximize student's learning outcomes and more children should be given opportunities to lead and embrace their leadership identity.

Organizational Level

Leaders and Organizational Culture

This study found that good listening and communicating skills are highly valued leadership behaviors exhibited in servant and friendship leadership. This suggests organizational managers and leaders should maximize these skills and intervene in the process of creating a listening supportive organizational culture that values individuals. Even though this process may be more difficult for traditional organizations compared to new start-ups, it can be started with one part of the organization before applying to the whole organization.

Leadership Development Program

This study reflects leadership development as a multilevel, multicontext, longitudinal social process, which suggests leadership programs should have multilateral approaches integrated with social activities.

First, as leadership development started from the early age, the programs should start by discovering which individuals have learned about leadership and the way they learn best in general (e.g., reading or listening). This helps to identify their current behaviors and belief patterns and indicates which patterns should be deconstructed, reconstructed, or reinforced.

Second, leadership development programs should incorporate multiple perspectives (e.g., coaching, mentoring, self-reflection, experimental projects, teamwork, building an organizational culture, and sports activity) over long periods of time, such as 13-week time span [107].

Third, leadership development programs should be embedded in social networks to provide social interactions, emotional and business supports to individuals. As creating social networks is leadership itself, it is important to encourage entrepreneurs—especially successful entrepreneurs—to create networks to support younger generations practice their leadership.

Leadership development programs for corporations and SMEs should not be considered the same, due to the different characteristics of the two. For example, entrepreneurs lack time and space because they remain synonymous with the business [84] and they play many roles, in particular, managerial and leadership roles while running their businesses [70]. As the preference in having flexibility and autonomy of entrepreneurs, leadership programs for SMEs should emphasize creating harmonized networks for entrepreneurs to exchange ideas, advice, and feedback from other successful entrepreneurs and leaders, instead of using formal practices such as classroom study.

There have been various effective leadership development programs such as LEAD, which has been used for nearly 3,000 SMEs in the UK[108]. The program has some similar elements to the findings of this study: think tanks, experiential events, action learning, coaching and mentoring, business shadowing and exchanges, site visit to larger companies, and reflective learning sessions. Barnes et al. [108] also suggests its benefits in business growth and work–life balance. Even though the context maybe different, it would be an indication of the choice for leadership training of SMEs.

Policy Makers Level

Because the family is the root of leadership development, policy makers may positively influence parenting and teacher's influence on children by conducting training programs to effectively empower children's leadership potential. Moreover, policy makers should consider integrating leadership development curriculum into career development curriculum. Due to the interrelationship of family, education, organizations, and society on leadership development, policy makers should be the main actors to foster the collaboration between parents, schools, organizations, and society in the process of empowering children's leadership potential, for example, creating an educational campaign for students to learn through involving in or creating their own community.

Final Thoughts

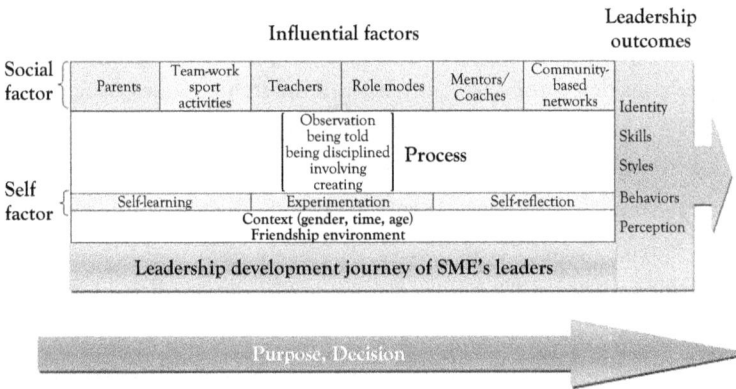

Figure 5.16 Framework of leadership development journey of SME's founder-owner

Leadership development is a self-development journey embedded in a social context (Figure 5.16). It is a multilevel, multicontext, longitudinal social development process. Multilevel includes individual, team, and community levels. Multicontext consists of family, school, employment, entrepreneurial, and community contexts. Longitudinal aspects imply that leadership development starts from early childhood and involves in daily life with different turning points created by one's decisions to avoid pain or gain pleasure. Leadership development outcomes overtime include perceptions, behaviors, skills, styles, and identity. The environment where leadership exercises the best is friendship. The drive of individual journey is the sense of purpose to grow or contribute to life.

The model found in this study suggests individuals, organizations, or society to construct their leadership development programs with the inclusions of both psychological and social factors.

- The process of gaining self-awareness through self-learning and self-reflection process should be prioritized. Individuals should then be aware of their current patterns of styles, behaviors, identity, and then identify their long-term purpose and desirable identity.
- Individuals learn from social factors—mentors/coaches/role models to improve their skills, behaviors, identity
- Individuals experiment what they learn
- Individuals reflect upon what they learn and gain feedback to improve their development process
- Individuals live in a community-based social networks

(learning materials: books aesthetic materials such as Ted Talk, novels, art)

Leadership is a choice. Leadership is a journey. You just made a choice to join the journey of reading this book. Give yourself sometimes to reflect upon the journey and design the next step for it.

References

[1] Bandura, A. 1977. *Social Learning Theory.* New York, NY: General Learning Press.

[2] Allen, S.J. 2007. "Adult Learning Theory & Leadership Development." *Leadership Review* 7, pp. 26–37.

[3] Burch, J. 1986. *Entrepreneurship.* New York, NY: John Wiley.

[4] Olakitan, O.O., and A.P. Ayobami. 2011. "An Investigation of Personality on Entrepreneurial Success." *Journal of Emerging Trends in Economics and Management Sciences* 2, no. 2, pp. 95–103.

[5] Kirkwood, J. 2007. "Igniting the Entrepreneurial Spirit: Is the Role Parents Play Gendered?" *International Journal of Entrepreneurial Behavior & Research* 13, no. 1, pp. 39–59.

[6] Kempster, S., and J. Cope. 2010. "Learning to Lead in the Entrepreneurial Context." *International Journal of Entrepreneurial Behavior & Research* 16, no. 1, pp. 5–34.

[7] Santrock, J.W. 2010. *Adolescence,* 13th ed. New York, NY: McGraw-Hill.

[8] Murphy, S.E., and S.K. Johnson. 2011. "The Benefits of a Long-lens Approach to Leader Development: Understanding the Seeds of Leadership." *The Leadership Quarterly* 22, no. 3, pp. 459–70.

[9] Baumrind, D. 1966. "Effects of Authoritative Parental Control on Child Behavior." *Child Development*, pp. 887–907.

[10] Baumrind, D. 1991. "The Influence of Parenting Style on Adolescent Competence and Substance Use." *The Journal of Early Adolescence* 11, no. 1, pp. 56–95.

[11] Steinberg, L., and A.S. Morris. 2001. "Adolescent Development." *Annual Review of Psychology* 52, no. 1, pp. 83–110.

[12] Avolio, B.J., M. Rotundo, and F.O. Walumbwa. 2009. "Early Life Experiences and Environmental Factors as Determinants of Leadership Emergence: The Role of Parental Influence and Rule Breaking Behavior." *The Leadership Quarterly* 20, pp. 329–42.

[13] Schmidtt-Rodermund, E. 2004. "Pathways to Successful Entrepreneurship: Parenting, Personality, Early Entrepreneurial Competence, and Interests." *Journal of Vocational Behavior* 65, pp. 498–518. doi:10.1016/j.jvb.2003.10.007

[14] Bandura, A. 2008. "The Reconstrual of 'Free Will' from the Agentic Perspective of Social Cognitive Theory." *Are We Free*, pp. 86–127.

[15] Avolio, B.J., F.O. Walumbwa, and T.J. Weber. 2009. "Leadership: Current Theories, Research, and Future Directions." *Annual Review of Psychology* 60, pp. 421–49.

[16] Schmitt, D.P., L. Alcalay, M. Allensworth, J. Allik, L. Ault, I. Austers, K.L. Bennett, G. Bianchi, F. Boholst, M.A.B. Cunen, and J. Braeckman. 2004. "Patterns and Universals of Adult Romantic Attachment Across 62 Cultural Regions: Are Models of Self and of Other Pancultural Constructs?" *Journal of Cross-Cultural Psychology* 35, no. 4, pp. 367–402.

[17] Arvey, R.D., M. Rotundo, W. Johnson, Z. Zhang, and M. McGue. 2006. "The Determinants of Leadership Role Occupancy: Genetic and Personality Factors." *The Leadership Quarterly* 17, no. 1, pp. 1–20.

[18] Arvey, R.D., Z. Zhang, B.J. Avolio, and R.F. Krueger. 2007. "Developmental and Genetic Determinants of Leadership Role Occupancy Among Women." *Journal of Applied Psychology* 92, no. 3, p. 693.

[19] Murphy, S.E., and S.K. Johnson. 2011. "The Benefits of a Long-lens Approach to Leader Development: Understanding the Seeds of Leadership." *The Leadership Quarterly* 22, no. 3, pp. 459–70.

[20] DeMoulin, D.F. 2002. "Examining the Impact of Extra-curricular Activities on the Personal Development of 149 High School Seniors." *Journal of Instructional Psychology* 29, no. 4, pp. 297–305.

[21] Aries, E., D. McCarthy, P. Salovey, and M.R. Banaji. 2004. "A Comparison of Athletes and Non-athletes at Highly Selective Colleges: Academic Performance and Personal Development." *Research in Higher Education* 45, no. 6, pp. 577–602.

[22] Chelladurai, P. 2011. "Participation in Sport and Leadership Development." In *Early Development and Leadership: Building the Next Generation of Leaders*, eds. S.E. Murphy and R.J. Reichard, 95–113. New York, NY: Psychology Press/Routledge.

[23] Fine, G.A. 1987. *With the Boys: Little League Baseball and Preadolescent Culture*. University of Chicago Press.

[24] Danish, S.J., A.J. Petitpas, and B.D. Hale. 1990. "Sport as a Context for Developing Competence." *Developing Social Competency in Adolescence* 3, pp. 169–94.

[25] Blinde, E.M., and S.L. Greendorfer. 1992. "Conflict and the College Sport Experience of Women Athletes." *Women in Sport and Physical Activity Journal* 1, no. 1, pp. 97–113.

[26] Kim, M.S. 1992. "Types of Leadership and Performance Norms of School Athletic Teams." *Perceptual and Motor Skills* 74, no. 3, pp. 803–06.

[27] Huntrods, C.S., B.P. An, and E.T. Pascarella. 2017. "Impact of Intercollegiate Athletic Participation on Leadership Development." *Journal of College Student Development* 58, no. 2, p. 198.

[28] Glassman, N.S., and S.M. Anderson. 1999. "Activating Transference Without Consciousness: Using Significant-other Representations to Go Beyond What Is Subliminally Given." *Journal of Personality and Social Psychology* 77, no. 6, pp. 1146–62.

[29] Andersen, S.M., and S. Chen. 2002. "The Relational Self: An Interpersonal Social-Cognitive Theory." *Psychological Review* 109, no. 4, p. 619.

[30] Baumrind, D. 1971. "Current Patterns of Parental Authority." *Developmental Psychology* 4, no. 1, p. 1.

[31] Chamundeswari, S. 2013. "Job Satisfaction and Performance of School Teachers." *International Journal of Academic Research in Business and Social Sciences* 3, no. 5, p. 420.

[32] Howell, J.M., and B.J. Avolio. 1992. "The Ethics of Charismatic Leadership: Submission or Liberation?" *Academy of Management Executive* 6, no. 2, pp. 43-54.

[33] Padilla, A., R. Hogan, and R.B. Kaiser. 2007. "The Toxic Triangle: Destructive Leaders, Susceptible Followers, and Conducive Environments." *The Leadership Quarterly* 18, no. 3, pp. 176–94.

[34] Schilling, J. 2009. "From Ineffectiveness to Destruction: A Qualitative Study on the Meaning of Negative Leadership." *Leadership* 5, no. 1, pp. 102–28.

[35] Schyns, B., and J. Schilling. 2013. "How Bad Are the Effects of Bad Leaders? A Meta-analysis of Destructive Leadership and Its Outcomes." *The Leadership Quarterly* 24, no. 1, pp. 138–58.

[36] Keupp, H., T. Ahbe, W. Gmür, R. Höfer, B. Mitzscherlich, W. Kraus, and F. Straus. 1999. *Identitätskonstruktionen*. Rowohlt-Taschenbuch-Verlag.

[37] Hogan, R., and R.B. Kaiser. 2005. "What We Know About Leadership." *Review of General Psychology* 9, no. 2, p. 169.

[38] Stone, A.G., R.F. Russell, and K. Patterson. 2004. "Transformational Versus Servant Leadership: A Difference in Leader Focus." *Leadership and Organization Development Journal* 25, pp. 349–61.

[39] Schwartz, T. 2010. "The Four Capacities Every Great Leader Needs." *Harvard Business Review*, available at http://blogs.hbr.org/schwartz/2010/10/the-four-capacities-every-grea.html (accessed February 20, 2010).

[40] Romero-Iribas, A.M., and C. Martínez-Priego. 2011. "Developing Leadership Through Education for Friendship." *Procedia-social and Behavioral Sciences*15, pp. 2248–52.

[41] Bradley, M.M. 2009. "Natural Selective Attention: Orienting and Emotion." *Psychophysiology* 46, no. 1, pp. 1–11.

[42] Nogueiras, G., E.S. Kunnen, and A. Iborra. 2017. "Managing Contextual Complexity in an Experiential Learning Course: A Dynamic Systems Approach through the Identification of Turning Points in Students' Emotional Trajectories." *Frontiers in Psychology* 8.

[43] Bird, B. 1989. *Entrepreneurial Behaviour, Glenview, Illinois*. Scott, Foresman & Company.

[44] Kempster, S. 2006. "Leadership Learning Through Lived Experience: A Process of Apprenticeship?" *Journal of Management & Organization* 12, no. 1, pp. 4–22.

[45] Schedlitzki, D., and G. Edwards. 2014. *Studying Leadership: Traditional and Critical Approaches*. Sage Publications.

[46] Ellemers, N., D. De Gilder, and S. Alexander Haslam. 2004. "Motivating Individuals and Groups at Work: A Social Identity Perspective on Leadership and Group Performance." *Academy of Management Review* 29, no. 3, pp. 459–78.

[47] Schein, E.H. 1985. *Organisational Culture and Leadership: A Dynamic View*. San Francisco: Jossey-Bass.

[48] Garavan, T., S. Watson, R. Carbery, and F. O'Brien. 2016. "The Antecedents of Leadership Development Practices in SMEs: The Influence of HRM Strategy and Practice." *International Small Business Journal* 34, no. 6, pp. 870–90.

[49] Dziczkowski, J. July 2013. "Mentoring and Leadership Development." In *The Educational Forum* (Vol. 77, No. 3, pp. 351–60). Taylor & Francis Group.

[50] Greenleaf, J.P., K. Klaus, and J. Arensdorf. 2017. "Cultivating Leadership Development: A Comprehensive Program for Undergraduates." *Journal of Leadership Education* 16, no. 1.

[51] Goleman, D., R.E. Boyatzis, and A. McKee. 2002. *The New Leaders: Transforming the Art of Leadership into the Science of Results*, 14. London: Little, Brown.

[52] Northouse, P.G. 2018. *Leadership: Theory and practice*. Sage Publications.

[53] Gladstone, M.S. 1988. *Mentoring: A Strategy for Learning in a Rapidly Changing Society*. Research and Development Secretariat at John Abbott College, PO Box 2000, Ste. Anne de Bellevue, Quebec, H9X 3L9, Canada.

[54] Sosik, J.J., V.M. Godshalk, and F.J. Yammarino. 2004. "Transformational Leadership, Learning Goal Orientation, and Expectations for Career Success in Mentor–Protégé Relationships: A Multiple Levels of Analysis Perspective." *The Leadership Quarterly* 15, no. 2, pp. 241–61.

[55] Kram, K.E., and L.A. Isabella. 1985. "Mentoring Alternatives: The Role of Peer Relationships in Career Development." *Academy of Management Journal* 28, no. 1, pp. 110–32.

[56] Gil, A.J., and F.J. Carrillo. 2016. "Knowledge Transfer and the Learning Process in Spanish Wineries." *Knowledge Management Research & Practice* 14, no. 1, pp. 60–68.

[57] Utrilla, P.N.C., F.A. Grande, and D. Lorenzo. 2015. "The Effects of Coaching in Employees and Organizational Performance: The Spanish Case." *Intangible Capital* 11, no. 2, pp. 166–89.

[58] Kampa-Kokesch, S., and M.Z. Anderson. 2001. "Executive Coaching: A Comprehensive Review of the Literature." *Consulting Psychology Journal: Practice and Research* 53, no. 4, p. 205.

[59] Colomo-Palacios, R., and C. Casado-Lumbreras. 2006. *Mentoring & Coaching: It Perspective.*

[60] Hannafey, F.T., and L.A. Vitulano. 2013. "Ethics and Executive Coaching: An Agency Theory Approach." *Journal of Business Ethics* 115, no. 3, pp. 599–603.

[61] Sue-Chan, C., and G.P. Latham. 2004. "The Relative Effectiveness of External, Peer, and Self-Coaches." *Applied Psychology* 53, no. 2, pp. 260–78.

[62] Pesso, T. 2005. *Self-coaching Method and System.* U.S. Patent Application 11/155,795.

[63] Losch, S., E. Traut-Mattausch, M.D. Mühlberger, and E. Jonas. 2016. "Comparing the Effectiveness of Individual Coaching, Self-coaching, and Group Training: How Leadership Makes the Difference." *Frontiers in Psychology* 7, p. 629.

[64] Ed Batista 2017. Self-Coaching: An Overview. [online] available at: http://edbatista.com/2013/07/self-coaching-an-overview.html (accessed July 7, 2017).

[65] Phillips, J.J., and L. Schmidt. 2012. *The Leadership Scorecard.* Routledge.

[66] Aldrich, H., and C. Zimmer. 1986. "Entrepreneurship Through Social Networks." *The Art and Science of Entrepreneurship*, 3–23. Cambridge, MA: Ballinger.

[67] Hoang, H., and B. Antoncic. 2003. "Network-based Research in Entrepreneurship: A Critical Review." *Journal of Business Venturing* 18, no. 2, pp. 165–87.

[68] Macpherson, A., O. Jones, and A. Kofinas. April 2008. "Making Sense of Mediated Learning in Small Firms." *Proceedings of the 3rd Organizational Knowledge, Learning and Capabilities Conference.* Copenhagen.

[69] Edwards, G. 2011. "Concepts of Community: A Framework for Contextualizing Distributed Leadership." *International Journal of Management Reviews* 13, no. 3, pp. 301–12.

[70] Fuller-Love, N. 2006. "Management Development in Small Firms." *International Journal of Management Reviews* 8, no. 3, pp. 175–90.

[71] Greve, A., and J.W. Salaff. 2003. "Social Networks and Entrepreneurship." *Entrepreneurship Theory and Practice* 28, no. 1, pp. 1–22.

[72] Shane, S., and D. Cable. 2002. "Network Ties, Reputation, and the Financing of New Ventures." *Management Science* 48, no. 3, pp. 364–81.

[73] Cullen-Lester, K.L., C.K. Maupin, and D.R. Carter. 2017. "Incorporating Social Networks into Leadership Development: A Conceptual Model and Evaluation of Research and Practice." *The Leadership Quarterly* 28, no. 1, pp. 130–52.

[74] Day, D.V. 2000. "Leadership Development: A Review in Context." *The Leadership Quarterly* 11, no. 4, pp. 581–613.

[75] Nowell, B., and N.M. Boyd. 2014. "Sense of Community Responsibility in Community Collaboratives: Advancing a Theory of Community as Resource and Responsibility." *American Journal of Community Psychology* 54, nos. 3–4, pp. 229–42.

[76] Shane, S., L. Kolvereid, and P. Westhead. 1991. "An Exploratory Examination of the Reasons Leading to New Firm Formation Across Country and Gender." *Journal of Business Venturing* 6, no. 6, pp. 431–46.

[77] Martiskainen, M. 2017. "The Role of Community Leadership in the Development of Grassroots Innovations." *Environmental Innovation and Societal Transitions* 22, pp. 78–89.

[78] Ford, J. 2010. "Studying Leadership Critically: A Psychosocial Lens on Leadership Identities." *Leadership* 6, no. 1, pp. 47–65.

[79] Ford, J., N. Harding, and M. Learmonth. 2008. *Leadership as Identity: Constructions and Deconstructions.* Springer.

[80] Rook, K.S. 1984. "The Negative Side of Social Interaction: Impact on Psychological Well-being." *Journal of Personality and Social Psychology* 46, no. 5, p. 1097.

[81] Labianca, G., and D.J. Brass. 2006. "Exploring the Social Ledger: Negative Relationships and Negative Asymmetry in Social Networks in Organizations." *Academy of Management Review* 31, no. 3, pp. 596–614.

[82] Chiu, C.Y.C., P. Balkundi, and F.J. Weinberg. 2017. "When Managers Become Leaders: The Role of Manager Network Centralities, Social Power, and Followers' Perception of Leadership." *The Leadership Quarterly* 28, no. 2, pp. 334–48.

[83] Sun, J., X. Chen, and S. Zhang. 2017. "A Review of Research Evidence on the Antecedents of Transformational Leadership." *Education Sciences* 7, no. 1, p. 15.

[84] Cope, J. 2003. "Entrepreneurial Learning and Critical Reflection: Discontinuous Events as Triggers for 'Higher-level' Learning." *Management Learning* 34, no. 4, pp. 429–50.

[85] Sparrowe, R.T. 2005. "Authentic Leadership and the Narrative Self." *The Leadership Quarterly* 16, no. 3, pp. 419–39.

[86] Clarke, J., R. Thorpe, L. Anderson, and J. Gold. 2006. "It's All Action, It's All Learning: Action Learning in SMEs." *Journal of European Industrial Training* 30, no. 6, pp. 441–55.

[87] Rae, D. 2000. "Understanding Entrepreneurial Learning: A Question of How?" *International Journal of Entrepreneurial Behaviour and Research* 6, no. 3, pp. 145–59.

[88] Kempster, S., B. Jackson, and M. Conroy. 2011. "Leadership as Purpose: Exploring the Role of Purpose in Leadership Practice." *Leadership* 7, no. 3, pp. 317–34.

[89] Bass, B.M., and R.M. Stogdill. 1990. *Bass & Stogdill's Handbook of Leadership: Theory, Research, and Managerial Applications.* Simon and Schuster.

[90] Hunt, J.G.J., and J.A. Conger. 1999. "From Where We Sit: An Assessment of Transformational and Charismatic Leadership Research." *The Leadership Quarterly.*

[91] Minton, J., R. Shaw, M.A. Green, L. Vanderbloemen, F. Popham, and G. McCartney. 2017. "Visualising and Quantifying 'Excess Deaths' in Scotland Compared With the Rest of the UK and the Rest of Western Europe." *J Epidemiol Community Health*, pp. jech-2016.

[92] Elder, Jr., G.H., and R.C. Rockwell. 1976. "Marital Timing in Women's Life Patterns." *Journal of Family History* 1, no. 1, pp. 34–53.

[93] Hagestad, G.O., and L.M. Burton. 1986. "Grandparenthood, Life Context, and Family Development." *American Behavioral Scientist* 29, no. 4, pp. 471–84.

[94] Day, D.V., J.W. Fleenor, L.E. Atwater, R.E. Sturm, and R.A. McKee. 2014. "Advances in Leader and Leadership Development: A Review of 25 Years of Research and Theory." *The Leadership Quarterly* 25, no. 1, pp. 63–82.

[95] Clapp-Smith, R., G.R. Vogelgesang, and J.B. Avey. 2009. "Authentic Leadership and Positive Psychological Capital: The Mediating Role of Trust at the Group Level of Analysis." *Journal of Leadership & Organizational Studies* 15, no. 3, pp. 227–40.

[96] Harms, P.D., S.M. Spain, and S.T. Hannah. 2011. "Leader Development and the Dark Side of Personality." *The Leadership Quarterly* 22, no. 3, pp. 495–509.

[97] Floyd, A. 2012. "'Turning Points' The Personal and Professional Circumstances that Lead Academics to Become Middle Managers." *Educational Management Administration & Leadership* 40, no. 2, pp. 272–84.

[98] Van der Maas, H.L., and P.C. Molenaar. 1992. "Stagewise Cognitive Development: An Application of Catastrophe Theory." *Psychological Review* 99, no. 3, p. 395.

[99] Granott, N., and J. Parziale, eds. 2002. *Microdevelopment: Transition Processes in Development and Learning,* 7 vols. Cambridge university press.

[100] Frijda, N.H. 1988. "The Laws of Emotion." *American Psychologist* 43, no. 5, p. 349.

[101] Lazarus, R.S. 1991. "Progress on a Cognitive-Motivational-Relational Theory of Emotion." *American Psychologist* 46, no. 8, p. 819.

[102] Solomon, C.B. 2007. *The Relationships Among Middle Level Leadership, Teacher Commitment, Teacher Colllective Efficacy, and Student Achievement* (Doctoral dissertation, University of Missouri-Columbia).

[103] Teruya, C., and Y.I. Hser. 2010. "Turning Points in the Life Course: Current Findings and Future Directions in Drug Use Research." *Current Drug Abuse Reviews* 3, no. 3, pp. 189–95.

[104] Kunnen, E.S., H.A. Bosma, C.P. Van Halen, and M. Van der Meulen. 2001. "A Self-organizational Approach to Identity and Emotions: An Overview and Implications." *Identity and Emotion: Development Through Self-organization,* pp. 202–30.

[105] Hayes, S.C. 2015. "Making Sense of Spirituality." In *the Act in Context,* 68–82. Routledge.

[106] Jepson, D. 2009a. "Leadership Context: The Importance of Departments." *Leadership & Organization Development Journal* 30, no. 1, pp. 36–52.

[107] Day, D.V., and H.P. Sin. 2011. "Longitudinal Tests of an Integrative Model of Leader Development: Charting and Understanding Developmental Trajectories." *The Leadership Quarterly* 22, no. 3, pp. 545–60.

[108] Barnes, S., S. Kempster, and S. Smith. 2015. *Leading Small Business: Business Growth Through Leadership Development.* Edward Elgar Publishing.

Thanks Message to the Readers

The day I wrote these last pages was a year later since the day I conducted the research for this book. It has been an enjoyable journey and thankfully the end of it opens a new stage in my journey of empowering others to reach their leadership potential thanks to the lessons from all participated SME's leaders. Since I came back to Vietnam from the UK in 2018, I have started 2 projects to empower the leadership potential within individuals "CSpeaking Gym" and "Be the Leaders" (check out at jenvuhuong.com/cspeakinggym and jenvuhuong.com/betheleaders). I would also like to congratulate you for completing the journey of discovering the leadership development journey of SME's leaders through the journey of reading this book. Thank you for joining me to make the journey more meaningful! I believe and I know you have leadership potential within, just live up to it day by day, be the leader of your life and empower people around you to do the same so that we can make the world be a better place.

Now is the time to make a Decision to live with a Purpose by learning by your Self or from others, then Experiment what you learn and Reflect upon it for improvement. Now is the time to develop as a leader of your life.

With love,
Talk to you soon!

—Jen Vuhuong

Gratitude Moment

I am deeply grateful for my life's different golden tickets. I live each day to earn that gratitude and in my efforts to live on the passion of empowering people to reach their potential to make a difference in life.

This book is dedicated to my family and the mission of empowering the leadership potential in each individual to make a difference in life.

My eldest sister, Flower, my ANGEL, has a lovely family. She has two kids, a boy and a girl. She lives in a good living condition with her kind husband. She has been promoted in her job, just as her husband. She goes to work every day, and she passes by my family every day after finishing work. She texts me everyday. She smiles every time she hears my voice. She feels happy every time she thinks about how her sister is trying to become the person she is inspired to be, to make a difference in people's lives.

My other elder sister, Tomorrow, my MUST, has a beautiful family. She has a boy and going to have another child soon. She is happier than anyone else, not because she has a fancy job, but just simply because she loves it; she loves working as a seller in the market. Her husband is in a well-paid job, and their standard of living has improved day by day. She wakes up early to go to the market everyday, and prepares food for my parents everyday after finishing work. She texts me once or twice a week. She smiles every time she thinks of how her younger sister is trying to become the person she must be, to make all the best things happen for people's lives.

My elder brother, Development, my HERO, has a great family. He has a boy. He works for the government. He is loved by people whenever he organizes a charity event. He goes to work everyday. He goes fishing as a hobby sometimes. He smiles when fishing and thinking about fishing memories with me. He calls me once or twice a month. He smiles every time he thinks about how his younger sister is trying her best to find a hero inside herself to make a difference to her family, to the people around her, and to herself.

My parents are not worried as before, and are happier more than ever to be surrounded by all their grandchildren. They still work everyday. They sometimes call me. They smile when they think about their small child who has a huge burning desire to live for her family, and for the people around her.

I wake up every morning grateful that I am alive, with the vibrancy of nonstop living, loving, and giving. Despite the distance and time, my heart is always with my family.

To Edwin, I cannot express how much thankful and appreciative to your effort and time to edit and share ideas to improve the book. Without you, the publishing book journey would have not been going well.

Gareth Edwards deserves a significant credit here for inspiring my journey of studying about leadership topic. Thanks for his guidance, support and insightful knowledge. Dr. Vikas Kumar is also my gratitude thanks to his willingness to support me not only in academic studying but also in my career path since the first day I decided to write a book on leadership.

Stuart Doughty, Tony Robbins, and Brendon Burchard also deserve a great appreciation for inspiring me to share my message and stay in the journey of empowering people to make a difference in their lives.

I could not express how much appreciative I feel toward Chevening scholarship which gave me the chance to study in the UK to raise my academic and professional standard that is a great foundation for this book.

Last but not least, I truly appreciate all the participants who are SME's founder-owner-managers, scholars of Chevening program and leaders of Toastmasters International in the UK.

It is impossible to thank each and a single person I have met in my life who has inspired me to live with passion every moment of life, so I apologize to all my friends not listed here. I truly appreciate you!

About the Author

Jen Vuhuong (her full Vietnamese name is Vu Thi Huong) obtained a degree in Electronics and Telecommunications from Hanoi University of Science and Technology in Vietnam, an excellent master's degree in Business Innovation and Technology Management in Spain, and an excellent master's degree in International Management in the UK.

After being awarded a scholarship by Samsung Corporation in her final year at university, Jen dedicated two years to work for Samsung Electronics Vietnam as a project owner and an on-the-job trainer. In 2013, she went to Spain for her first master's degree with the world's top full scholarship—Erasmus. In 2014, she moved to work in Malaysia for a Dell partner for almost two years. In 2016, Jen devoted five months to work as an event manager for a bicycle and educational campaign of a Belgian NGO in Vietnam. Later, Jen went to the UK and completed her second master's. Jen went back to Vietnam and participated in different education projects as a trainer, education development manager, business consultant and head of committee of Hanoi Entrepreneur Community.

Since 2011, Jen has worked on her own passion of empowering leaders and entrepreneurs to reach their potential to make a difference in the world through teaching soft skills, leading public speaking communities/personal development seminars/training workshops, and writing books in both Asia and Europe. Since then, Jen has started pursue her life career as a performance and leadership trainer, international management consultant, coach, and writer. Till 2017, Jen has published three books "Nonstop living, loving and giving," "The Goal Achiever: the ultimate nine steps to achieve a personal goal (particularly a full scholarship)," "Unleash your passion: the ultimate seven pillars toward full potential and fulfilment." She is currently working on three other book projects: a leadership book based on an empirical study over the past one year; 'The YOU journal' book based on a habit-based study; and a novel related to women leadership. Jen was awarded as the winner of International Public Speaking Contest in Malaysia and Vietnam in 2016 and 2018. She has been an awarded speaker at different speaking events such as Enterprise conference in Hue University in Vietnam or Collaborative leadership conference in Bradford University in the UK.

Jen is thankful for the different opportunities to continue living, to being loved unconditionally, and to have received all the best things. She has been amazed by every single person she has met who has lived fully, loved completely, and given devotedly. She has been inspired to be non-stop living, loving, and giving every moment of her life and as a duty to inspire people around her to do so.

Meet Jen online and get deeper training on leadership development at jenvuhuong.com/leadershipdevelopment or email to jenvuhuong@gmail.com

Index

active listening, 80–81
Anderson, M. Z., 55
authoritative leadership, 47–49
authoritative parenting, 44–45

bad role model, 49
Bass, B. M., 6
behavioral development, 79

Cambridge Dictionary, 68
Carrillo, F. J., 55
Chamundeswari, S., 48
Chavis, D. M., 8
Choi, J., 32
coaching, 55
communication, 82
community-based networks, 56–60
community leadership, 8–9
contingency leadership theories, 5–6
Cope, J., 21–22, 24–25, 32, 44, 51

Dean, H., 25
decision, 73–78
distributed leadership, 7–9

effective listening, 80
effective self-learning, 64–66, 69–70
emotions, 50–51
emphasizing contextual variables, 8
empirical evidence, 32
entrepreneurial leadership
    entrepreneurship and leadership, 20
    evolution, 22–25
    overview, 19–22
entrepreneurs, 19, 21–22, 44, 51,
        59, 85
entrepreneurship and leadership,
        20–21
environment, leadership development,
        82–83
experience and leaning, 30

family and school level, 83–84
Fieldler's theory, 5–6
Ford, J., 25, 59

Gil, A. J., 55
good role model, 50

Havard Business Review, 68
Hooijberg, R., 32

identity development, 79
implicit theory, 10
influential factors
    authoritative leadership, 47–49
    bad role model, 49
    coaching, 55
    community-based networks, 56–60
    emotions, 50–51
    good role model, 50
    influence of parents, 43–45
    leadership quality, 43
    mentoring, 52–54
    organizational culture, 51–52
    social factors, 42
    teachers, 47
    teamwork, 45–47
interpersonal approach, 30–31
interview process, 39–40

Jepson, D., 10–11
Johnson, S. K., 46

Kampa-Kokesch, S., 55
Kempster, S., 21–22, 24–25, 32, 44,
        51
Kim, M. S., 46
Kirkwood, J., 44

leaders and organizational culture, 84
leadership
    definition, 1–2

development, 29–34
distributed, 7–9
entrepreneurial, 20–25
implicit and social identity theory,
    10
overview, 1–4
process of, 31–34
traditional approaches to, 4–7,
    30–31
leadership development in SME
    evolution, 22–25
    overview, 19–22
leadership development program,
    84–85
Leitch, C. M., 21, 22
life course approach, 74
listening, 79–80

McMillan, D. W., 8
Martiskainen, M., 9
mentoring, 52–54
mindset, 30
moral, 30
Murphy, S. E., 46

nonverbal communication, 82

organizational culture, 51–52
organizational level, 84–85

parenting styles, 44–45
personal development, 52
perspective development, 79
policy makers level, 85–86
process approach, 6–7
process of leadership, 31–34
psychological factors
    experimentation, 66–67
    massive advocate, 61
    self-learning, 61–66
    self-reflection, 67–70
purpose, 70–73

quality, leadership, 43

role models, 49–52

Santrock, J. W., 44
self-development, 30
self-efficacy, 45, 62
self-efficiency, 30
self factors, 41, 42
self-learning, 61–66
self-reflection, 67–70
skills development, 79
small and medium-sized enterprises
    (SMEs), 19, 33. See also
    leadership development in
    SME
    interview process, 39–40
    philosophies and approaches,
        37–38
    strategy, 38
social factors, 41, 42
social identity theory, 10
social learning theory, 43
static approach, 30–31
strategic listening, 81
style and skill theories, 5

Taylor, M., 8
teachers styles, 47–49
teamwork, 45–47
360-degree feedback, 31–32
traditional leadership, 4–7, 30–31
trait theories, 4–5
transformational leadership, 6
TRIGGERS, 73–74

Vecchio, R. P., 20–21
verbal communication, 82
Volery, T, 21, 22

Zeldtich, Morris, 53

OTHER TITLES IN THE ENTREPRENEURSHIP AND SMALL BUSINESS MANAGEMENT COLLECTION

Scott Shane, Case Western University, Editor

- *Open Innovation Essentials for Small and Medium Enterprises: A Guide to Help Entrepreneurs in Adopting the Open Innovation Paradigm in Their Business* by Luca Escoffier, Adriano La Vopa, Phyllis Speser, and Daniel Satinsky
- *The Technological Entrepreneur's Playbook* by Ian Chaston
- *Licensing Myths & Mastery: Why Most Ideas Don't Work and What to Do About It* by William S. Seidel
- *Arts and Entrepreneurship* by J. Mark Munoz and Julie Shields
- *The Human Being's Guide to Business Growth: A Simple Process for Unleashing the Power of Your People for Growth* by Gregory Scott Chambers
- *Understanding the Family Business: Exploring the Differences Between Family and Nonfamily Businesses, Second Edition* by Keanon J. Alderson

Announcing the Business Expert Press Digital Library

Concise e-books business students need for classroom and research

This book can also be purchased in an e-book collection by your library as

- a one-time purchase,
- that is owned forever,
- allows for simultaneous readers,
- has no restrictions on printing, and
- can be downloaded as PDFs from within the library community.

Our digital library collections are a great solution to beat the rising cost of textbooks. E-books can be loaded into their course management systems or onto students' e-book readers. The **Business Expert Press** digital libraries are very affordable, with no obligation to buy in future years. For more information, please visit **www.businessexpertpress.com/librarians**. To set up a trial in the United States, please email **sales@businessexpertpress.com**.